Palgrave Studies in Democracy, Innovation, and Entrepreneurship for Growth

Series Editor

Elias G. Carayannis, PhD
School of Business
George Washington University
Washington, DC, USA

The central theme of this series is to explore why some geographic areas grow and others stagnate over time, and to measure the effects and implications in a trans-disciplinary context that takes both historical evolution and geographical location into account. In other words, when, how, and why does the nature and dynamic of a political regime inform and shape the drivers of growth and especially innovation and entrepreneurship? In this socio-economic, socio-political, and socio-technical context, how could we best achieve growth, financially and environmentally? This series aims to address key questions framing policy and strategic decision-making at firm, industry, national, and regional levels, such as:

- How does technological advance occur, and what are the strategic processes and institutions involved?
- How are new businesses created? To what extent is intellectual property protected?
- Which cultural characteristics serve to promote or impede innovation?
- In what ways is wealth distributed or concentrated?

A primary feature of the series is to consider the dynamics of innovation and entrepreneurship in the context of globalization, with particular respect to emerging markets, such as China, India, Russia, and Latin America. (For example, what are the implications of China's rapid transition from providing low-cost manufacturing and services to becoming an innovation powerhouse? How sustainable financially, technologically, socially, and environmentally will that transition prove? How do the perspectives of history and geography explain this phenomenon?)
Contributions from researchers in a wide variety of fields will connect and relate the relationships and inter-dependencies among

- Innovation,
- Political Regime, and
- Economic and Social Development.

We will consider whether innovation is demonstrated differently across sectors (e.g., health, education, technology) and disciplines (e.g., social sciences, physical sciences), with an emphasis on discovering emerging patterns, factors, triggers, catalysts, and accelerators to innovation, and their impact on future research, practice, and policy. This series will delve into what are the sustainable and sufficient growth mechanisms for the foreseeable future for developed, knowledge-based economies and societies (such as the EU and the US) in the context of multiple, concurrent, and inter-connected "tipping-point" effects with short (MENA) as well as long (China, India) term effects from a geo-strategic, geo-economic, geo-political, and geo-technological (GEO-STEP) set of perspectives. This conceptualization lies at the heart of the series, and offers to explore the correlation between democracy, innovation, and entrepreneurship for growth. Proposals should be sent to Elias Carayannis at caraye@gwu.edu.

More information about this series at
http://www.springer.com/series/14635

Manlio Del Giudice • Maria Rosaria Della Peruta

The Satisfaction of Change

How Knowledge and Innovation Overcome Loyalty in Decision-Making Processes

palgrave
macmillan

Manlio Del Giudice
International Business Administration
Link Campus University International
Business Administration
Naples, Italy

Maria Rosaria Della Peruta
Faculty of Economics
Second University of Naples Faculty of
Economics
Naples, Italy

Palgrave Studies in Democracy, Innovation, and Entrepreneurship for Growth
ISBN 978-3-319-41883-4 ISBN 978-3-319-41884-1 (eBook)
DOI 10.1007/978-3-319-41884-1

Library of Congress Control Number: 2016955558

Printed on acid-free paper

This Palgrave Macmillan imprint is published by Springer Nature
The registered company is Springer International Publishing AG Switzerland
The registered company address is: Gewerbestrasse 11, 6330 Cham, Switzerland

Contents

List of Figures

List of Tables

CHAPTER 1

Introduction

Customer loyalty has long time been a topic which has drawn much attention within the academic management literature (Chandrashekaran, Rotte, Tax, & Grewal, 2007; Palmatier, Scheer, & Steenkamp, 2007; Yim, Tse, & Chan, 2008). Heightened competitive dynamics in contexts characterized by high business intensity and oversupply (Bang & Joshi, 2010; 2002a, 2002b; Schindehutte, Morris, & Kocak, 2008; Sirmon, Hitt, Arregle, & Campbell, 2010), the evolution of types of competition (Adler, 2010), the progressive saturation of many markets, and the structural modifications of the exchange processes induced by the emergence of the digital economy (Gnyawali, Fan, & Penner, 2010; Wind & Mahajan, 2001; Straub, Hoffman, Weber & Steinfield, 2002; Straub, Hoffman, Weber & Steinfield, 2002b; Palacios-Marqués, Merigó & Soto-Acosta, 2015a, Palacios-Marqués, Soto-Acosta & Merigó, 2015b) have sustained the progressive importance of the topic in recent years, leading to a growing interest of scholars primarily for the interconnections between offer and demand, as a direct consequence of the increasing technological, competitive, and relational complexity that permeates the markets (Brondoni, 2002a, 2002b; Carayannis, 1998, 1999, 2008, 2009, 2013; Carayannis & Alexander, 1999, 2002; Carayannis & Campbell, 2009, 2011; Chung, Jin, & Sternquist, 2007). Moreover, understanding that the "customer theory" and the behavioral patterns of demand had not given adequate insight into the phenomena resulting from purchase decisions and the evaluation of repurchase options was previously pointed out by several

M. Del Giudice, M.R. Della Peruta, *The Satisfaction of Change*,
DOI 10.1007/978-3-319-41884-1_1

researchers (Berger, Möslein, Piller, & Reichwald, 2005; Day & Wensley, 1983; Grönroos, 1994a, 1994b). However, only more recently, the study of demand behavior has shown that the extension of research to product–customer interaction subsequent to a purchase is to be considered fundamental to generate new knowledge on a core construct such as customer loyalty (Ball, Coelho, & Machás, 2004; Gijsbrechts, Heerde, & Pauwels, 2008; Tse, Nicosia, & Wilton, 1991; Van Heerde & Bijmolt, 2005).

The dyscrasic trade-off inherent in customer behavior, in the words of Hirschmann between "wanting to be faithful" and "having to be faithful", has inextricably marked a boundary between the objectives of loyalty management, driving firms toward the need of making choices: to conquer new consumers, accepting a higher turnover of the customer portfolio, or retain existing customers, minimizing their churn rate and stimulating retention, to aim at a higher marginal revenue? Increased market volatility, uncertainty, the rapid change that characterizes economic and social scenarios, and the fast "evolution" of online markets, as opposed to the more static nature of offline markets, have revealed some insights directing this work of research toward the second option (Selden & MacMillan, 2006; Tsai, 2005; Verhees, Meulenberg, & Pennings, 2010; Vrontis & Thrassou, 2007). Our research starts from the assumption that online markets, having more points of friction and greater dynamism than the classic ones, have led to a redefinition of the concept of loyalty and the topics related to it (Shankar, Smith, & Rangaswamy, 2003; Shapiro & Varian, 1999, Varian, 2000; Zhang & He, 2012).

The growth of the cognitive power and a greater eclecticism of customers, their more marked propensity to '"disloyalty", the affirmation of individual consumption patterns toward the search of demand demassification, the gradual increase in consumer expectations toward the offer, and the increasing and changing interconnection between offer and demand have led to outlining the features of a potentially dynamic relationship between the business system and the customer (Brown & Eisenhardt, 1997; Iansiti & West, 1997; Ravasi & Verona, 2001; Sawney & Prandelli, 2000; Srinivasan & Hanssens, 2009; Villanueva & Hanssens, 2007).

The research design identifies in this scenario the latent assumptions in the developed model (Greenacre, 2007; Greenacre & Blasius, 2006). The basic hypothesis is related to the concept of shopping script: customers continuously experiencing online purchasing from the same supplier develop a behavioral pattern, precisely a script, able to reduce their cognitive effort and optimize purchase time. The creation of this script, however, is also induced by the structural design of the supplier's website, which, through customer service tools, "would mark" a privileged path for loyal customers, in order to allow them to manage purchases easier and faster, thanks to the exploitation of a cognitive scheme (Brüggen, Foubert, & Gremler, 2011; Hsu & Chiang, 2011; Jacobs & De Klerk, 2010; Sternee, 2000). The research hypothesis is that once a customer has become fully aware of the shopping script, he will be more reluctant to abandon his regular supplier. In other words, the possession of the script and the customer satisfaction inherent in its use will serve as factors of resistance to change by the customer. The model also takes into account the size of a possible limitation of this resistance: according to the instructions of the management literature, as "control variable" of the process the construct *willingness to pay more* is chosen, that is, the voluntary attitude of a customer to pay more for the products of the supplier of reference so as to retain the use of the acquired shopping script (Xu, Goedegebuure, & van der Heijden, 2006; Zeithaml, Berry, & Parasuraman, 1996). In the present study, the validity of the model is tested in its entirety, right from the choice of the reference context; in order to double-check the assumptions underlying the research design, the choice was oriented toward a market with clearly defined structural features: high-intensity business, low cost of searching for alternative suppliers, interchangeability of products and suppliers, market transparency, low information asymmetries, and tendential consumer disloyalty. Therefore, the final decision has fallen on the digital market of computer and hi-tech products, with particular reference to business to business (B2B) (Le Meunier-FitzHugh & Lane, 2009; Lechner & Kreutzer, 2010; Lee, Huang, Barnes, & Kao, 2010; Lee & Kim, 2008; Masanell & Ricart, 2010; McGrath, 2010; O'Sullivan, 2010; Pil & Holweg, 2006). Thus, the first innovation of the model is to represent one of the very few empirical contributions focused on B2B, a particularly sensitive sector because of the structural features of the processes of purchase and consumption, and the actors involved (Hutt & Speh, 2012).

The work is organized as follows. The initial introductive analysis of the impact of the digital economy and the transformations in exchange processes is followed by an extensive review of the management and economic literature. Special attention is paid to the analysis of the theoretical constructs that constitute the research design: customer satisfaction, shopping experience, resistance to change, script theory, and loyalty. The main contributions and reflections drawn from the literature related to the size of the developed model are individually examined. The evidence and considerations derived from a meticulous and thorough study of the literature are followed by the definition of the model. In this context, the criteria for choosing the field of application of the assumptions and the possible correlation between the knowledge of a shopping script and voluntary resistance to change are introduced. Through the analysis of innovative Internet tools typically used in B2B to support customer retention (from profiling to customer service), the conditions for the study of the factors of emergence, management, and monitoring of shopping scripts are established. The initial assumption is that businesses operating in the world of Internet are unlikely to maintain a competitive advantage over time. The increasing availability of information and the increasing number of operators in several similar or adjacent fields and services have undermined the traditional customer loyalty to the producers of the Fordist economy. Moreover, the relationship of trust between supplier and customer, created by the salesperson in offline markets, and the look-and-feel sensation are suddenly disappearing in the economy of digital virtuality (in which the role of the salesperson is played indeed by the website, and the product is essentially virtualized). The consequence of this process, which is still in progress, is to be found in the behavior adopted by businesses toward a rethinking of the tools to support loyalty, giving space to new sensors capable of "listening to customers" and making them loyal. The theoretical assumptions of the developed model are in part drawn on classical economics, and in part on the management literature. In essence, the model proposes an analysis in a "digital" view of the economic theory of switching costs and the resulting lock-in mechanisms; in a classical economy, switching costs are a barrier (often negatively perceived) to disloyalty. A customer may paradoxically be "trapped" in a relationship, not so much by choice, but because of either economic convenience or difficulty or "induced" reluctance to change. In this sense, the switching cost would stimulate the behavioral dimension of loyalty, and not the cognitive, inducing opportunistic behavior on the part of the offer and generating dissatisfaction in customers, despite them being loyal (but only "behaviorally"). However, the underlying model of this study reverses such tendency through the study of knowledge by the business customer of a shopping script that maximizes its utility function, making the shopping expedition extremely rapid and satisfactory. The greatest difficulty induced by the higher churn rate on the Internet, and the minimization of search costs typical of the digital tool, has led us to define a particularly sophisticated model, integrating more functionalities on the

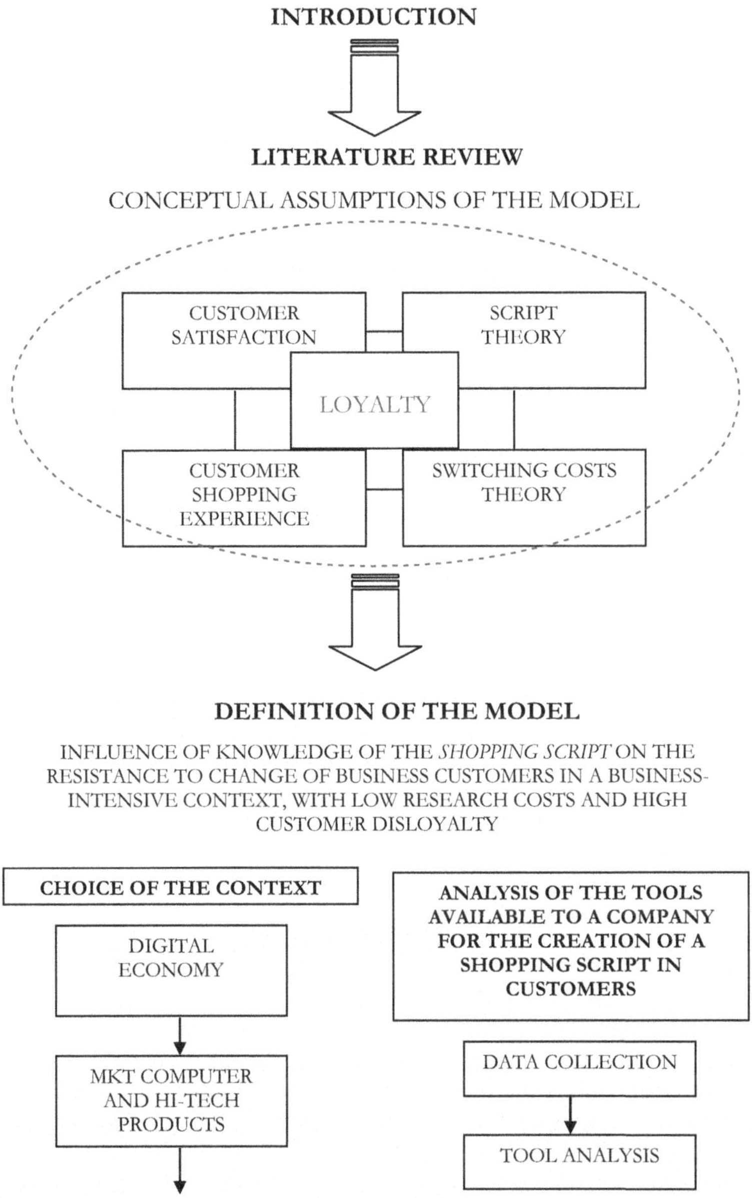

Fig. 1.1 Presentation of the research design

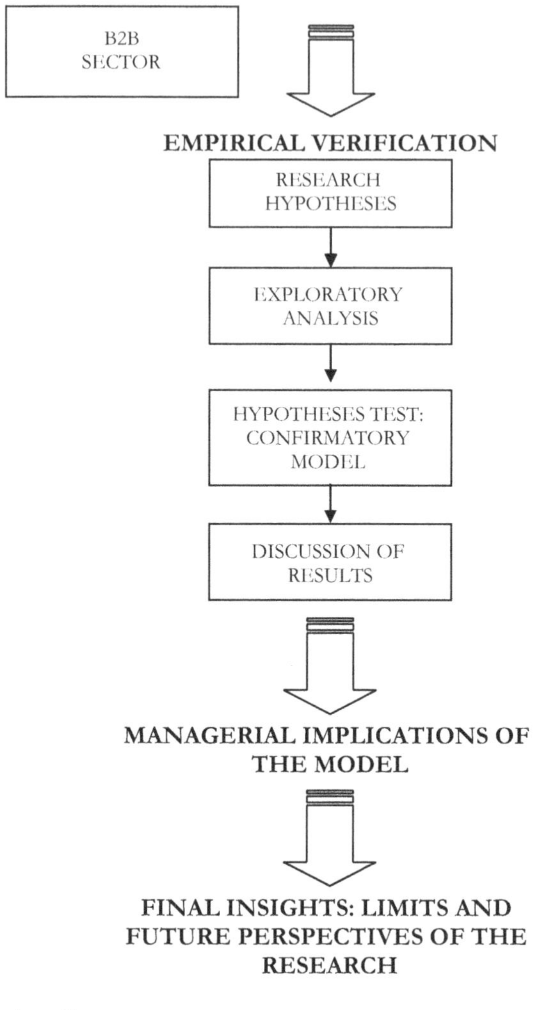

Fig. 1.1 (continued)

same website, toward the ultimate goal of loyalty satisfaction (synolon of behavioral and cognitive loyalty). The model provides an empirical analysis conducted on a purposive sample of a cluster of 280 companies in the hi-tech industry.[1] The definition of the hypotheses is conducted in parallel with the selection of scales/items. The empirical analysis starts from the selection of scales/items through a pilot test conducted with the methodology of in-depth interviews, supported by a bibliographical recognition of the literature. At this point, a more thorough selection of the identified items is developed (taking into account Cronbach's alpha [α] and composite reliability) and the hypotheses are tested through multiple tools of multivariate statistical analysis. The hypotheses are also tested through factor analysis: an exploratory analysis on a first data set of firms is followed by a confirmatory model on another data set, with the purpose of demonstrating the research hypotheses presented. As the proposed model aims at being a useful and effective tool for online businesses, its main managerial and strategic implications and its adaptability to existing contexts are discussed below. The work of this research concludes with some ideas for future research and the evidence of the limits attached to it.

In a very brief schematic synthesis, the complete model proposed in this study is presented in Fig. 1.1.

Note

1. As will be shown in Chap. 4, which is devoted to the empirical analysis, the sample was split into an exploratory data set consisting of 100 companies and a confirmatory data set consisting of 180 companies, in order to test the research hypotheses (returning, on the whole, 179 questionnaires). The research, however, included another 30 companies, involved in the in-depth interview and pre-test phases. To all managers of these companies, I feel bound to express my gratitude for their availability to respond to the questionnaire and provide valuable information for this study.

Bibliography

Adler, R. (2010). Enhancing business success: The role of performance management. *Business Horizons, 53*(4), 331–333.

Ball, D., Coelho, P. S., & Machás, A. (2004). The role of communication and trust in explaining customer loyalty: An extension to the ECSI model. *European Journal of Marketing, 38*(9/10), 1272–1293.

Ballestra L.V., Del Giudice M., Della Peruta M.R. (2014), An analysis of a model for the diffusion of engineering innovations under multi-firm competition, *International Journal of Technology Management, 66*(4), 346–357.

Bang, V. V., & Joshi, S. L. (2010). Market expansion strategy–performance relationship. *Journal of Strategic Marketing, 18*(1), 57–75.

Belkahla, W., & Triki, A. (2011). Customer knowledge enabled innovation capability: proposing a measurement scale. *Journal of knowledge management, 15*(4), 648–674.

Berger, C., Möslein, K., Piller, F., & Reichwald, R. (2005). Co-designing modes of cooperation at the customer interface: Learning from exploratory research. *European Management Review, 2*(1), 70–87.
Brondoni, S. M. (2002a). Global markets and market-space competition. *Symphonya. Emerging Issues in Management,* Issue 1.
Brondoni, S. M. (2002b). Overture in "Corporate culture and market complexity". *Symphonya. Emerging Issues in Management,* Issue 2.
Brown, S. L., & Eisenhardt, K. M. (1997). The art of continuous change: Linking complexity theory and time-paced evolution in relentlessly shifting organizations. *Administrative science quarterly,* 1–34.
Brüggen, E. C., Foubert, B., & Gremler, D. D. (2011). Extreme makeover: Short- and long-term effects of a remodeled servicescape. *Journal of Marketing, 75*(5), 71–87.
Carayannis, E. G. (1998). The strategic management of technological learning in project/program management: The role of extranets, intranets and intelligent agents in knowledge generation, diffusion, and leveraging. *Technovation, 18*(11), 697–703.
Carayannis, E. G. (1999). Knowledge transfer through technological hyperlearning in five industries. *Technovation, 19*(3), 141–161.
Carayannis, E. G. (2008). Knowledge-driven creative destruction, or leveraging knowledge for competitive advantage: Strategic knowledge arbitrage and serendipity as real options drivers triggered by co-opetition, co-evolution and co-specialization. *Industry & Higher Education, 22*(6), 1–11.
Carayannis, E. G. (2009). Firm evolution dynamics: Towards sustainable entrepreneurship and robust competitiveness in the knowledge economy and society. *International Journal of Innovation & Regional Development, 1*(3), 235–254.
Carayannis, E. G. (2013). Strategic knowledge arbitrage and serendipity (SKARSE) in action. *The Voice of Technology,* (Winter), 34–25.
Carayannis, E. G., & Alexander, J. (1999). Winning by co-opeting in strategic government-university-industry R&D partnerships: The power of complex, dynamic knowledge networks. *Journal of Technology Transfer, 24*(2–3), 197–210.
Carayannis, E. G., & Alexander, J. (2002). Is technological learning a firm core competence, when, how, and why? A longitudinal, multi-industry study of firm technological learning and market performance. *Technovation, 22*(10), 625–643.
Carayannis, E. G., & Campbell, D. F. (2009). 'Mode 3' and 'Quadruple Helix': Toward a 21st century fractal innovation ecosystem. *International Journal of Technology Management, 46*(3–4), 201–234.
Carayannis, E. G., & Campbell, D. F. (2011). Open innovation diplomacy and a 21st century fractal research, education and innovation (FREIE) ecosystem: Building on the quadruple and quintuple helix innovation concepts and the

'Mode 3' knowledge production system. *Journal of the Knowledge Economy, 2*(3), 327–372.

Chandrashekaran, M., Rotte, K., Tax, S. S., & Grewal, R. (2007). Satisfaction strength and customer loyalty. *Journal of Marketing Research, 44*(1), 153–163.

Chung, J., Jin, B., & Sternquist, B. (2007). The role of market orientation in channel relationships when channel power is imbalanced. *The International Review of Retail, Distribution and Consumer Research, 17*(2), 159–176.

Day, G. S., & Wensley, R. (1983). Marketing theory with a strategic orientation. *Journal of Marketing, 47*(4), 78–89.

Gijsbrechts, E., Heerde, H. J. v., & Pauwels, K. (2008). Winners and losers in a major price war. *Journal of Marketing Research, 45*(October), 499–518.

Gnyawali, D. R., Fan, W., & Penner, J. (2010). Competitive actions and dynamics in the digital age: An empirical investigation of social networking firms. *Information Systems Research, 21*, 594–613.

Greenacre, M. (2007). *Correspondence analysis in practice* (2nd ed.). Chapman & Hall/CRC Press.

Greenacre, M., & Blasius, J. (2006). *Multiple correspondence analysis and related methods*. Chapman & Hall/CRC Press.

Grönroos, C. (1994a). Quo Vadis marketing? Toward a relationship marketing approach. *Journal of Marketing Management, 10*, 347–360.

Grönroos, C. (1994b). From marketing mix to relationship marketing: Towards a paradigm shift in marketing. *Management Decision, 32*, 4–20.

Hsu, T., & Chiang, C. (2011). Script comparisons during service encounters in fast-food chains. *Tourism and Hospitality Research, 11*(January), 19–29.

Hutt, M. D., & Speh, T. W. (2012). *Business marketing management: B2B*. Cengage Learning.

Iansiti, M. and West, J. "Technology Integration: Turning Great Research into Great Products," *Harvard Business Review* (75:May-June) 1997, pp 69–79.

Jacobs, B., & De Klerk, H. M. (2010). Online apparel shopping behaviour of South African professional women: The role of consumers' apparel shopping scripts. *International Journal of Consumer Studies, 34*, 255–264.

Li, H., & Atuahene-Gima, K. (2001). The impact of interaction between R&D and marketing on new product performance: an empirical analysis of Chinese high technology firms. *International Journal of Technology Management, 21*(1-2), 61–75.

Le Meunier-FitzHugh, K., & Lane, N. (2009). Collaboration between sales and marketing, market orientation and business performance in business-to-business organizations. *Journal of Strategic Marketing, 17*(3), 291–306.

Lechner, C., & Kreutzer, M. (2010). Coordinating growth initiatives in multi-unit firms. *Long Range Planning, 43*(1), 6–32.

Lee, C., Huang, S., Barnes, F., & Kao, L. (2010). Business performance and customer relationship management: The effect of IT, organizational contingency

and business process on Taiwanese manufacturers. *Total Quality Management & Business Excellence, 21*(1), 43–65.
Lee, H. H., & Kim, J. (2008). The effects of shopping orientations on consumers' satisfaction with product search and purchases in a multi-channel environment. *Journal of Fashion Marketing and Management, 12*(2), 193–216.
Masanell, R. C., & Ricart, J. E. (2010). From strategy to business models and onto tactics. *Long Range Planning, 43*(2), 195–215.
McGrath, R. G. (2010). Business models: A discovery driven approach. *Long Range Planning, 43*(2), 247–261.
O'Sullivan, T. (2010). Dangling conversations: Web-forum use by a symphony orchestra's audience members. *Journal of Marketing Management, 26*(7), 656–670.
Palmatier, R. W., Scheer, L. K., & Steenkamp, J. B. E. M. (2007). Customer loyalty to whom? Managing the benefits and risks of salesperson-owned loyalty. *Journal of Marketing Research, 44*(2), 185–199.
Pil, F. K., & Holweg, M. (2006). Evolving from value chain to value grid. *Sloan Management Review, 47*(4), 72–80.
Ravasi, D., & Verona, G. (2001). Organising the process of knowledge integration: the benefits of structural ambiguity. *Scandinavian Journal of Management, 17*(1), 41–66.
Sawhney, M., & Prandelli, E. (2000). Communities of creation: managing distributed innovation in turbulent markets. *California management review, 42*(4), 24–54.
Schindehutte, M., Morris, M. H., & Kocak, A. (2008). Understanding market-driving behavior: The role of entrepreneurship. *Journal of Small Business Management, 46*(1), 4–26.
Selden, L., & MacMillan, I. C. (2006). Manage customer-centric innovation systematically. *Harvard Business Review, 84*(4), 108–116.
Shankar, V., Smith, A. K., & Rangaswamy, A. (2003). Customer satisfaction and loyalty in online and offline environments. *International Journal of Research in Marketing, 20*(2), 153–175.
Shapiro, C., & Varian, H. R. (1999). *Informatiom rules. A strategic guide to the network economy.* Boston: Harvard Business School Press.
Sirmon, D. G., Hitt, M. A., Arregle, J. L., & Campbell, J. T. (2010). The dynamic interplay of capability strengths and weaknesses: Investigating the bases of temporary competitive advantage. *Strategic Management Journal, 31*, 1386–1409.
Srinivasan, S., & Hanssens, D. M. (2009). Marketing and firm value: Metrics, methods, findings, and future directions. *Journal of Marketing research, 46*(3), 293–312.
Sternee, J. (2000). *Customer service on internet.* New York: John Wiley and Sons.
Taherparvar, N., Esmaeilpour, R., & Dostar, M. (2014). Customer knowledge management, innovation capability and business performance: a case study of the banking industry. *Journal of Knowledge Management, 18*(3), 591–610.

Tsai, S. P. (2005). Integrated marketing as management of holistic consumer experience. *Business Horizons, 48*(5), 431–441.

Tse, D. K., Nicosia, F., & Wilton, P. C. (1991). Consumer satisfaction as a process. *Psychology and Marketing, 7*(Fall), 177–193.

Van Heerde, H., & Bijmolt, T. H. A. (2005). Decomposing the promotional revenue bump for loyalty program members versus nonmembers. *Journal of Marketing Research, 42*(October), 443–457.

Varian, H. (2000). Markets for information goods. In *Monetary policy in a world of knowlege-based growth, quality change, and uncertain measurement*, Conference proceedings. Retrieved September 2004, from http://www.sims.berkeley.edu/~hal/Papers/japan/japan.pdf

Verhees, F. J. H. M., Meulenberg, M. T. G., & Pennings, J. M. E. (2010). Performance expectations of small firms considering radical product innovation. *Journal of Business Research, 63*(7), 772–777.

Villanueva, J., & Hanssens, D. M. (2007). Customer Equity: Measurement, Management and Research Opportunities. *Marketing, 1*(1), 1–95.

Vrontis, D., & Thrassou, A. (2007). A new conceptual framework for business-consumer relationships. *Marketing Intelligence & Planning, 25*(7), 789–806.

Wind, J., & Mahajan, V. (Eds.). (2001). *Digital marketing*. New York: Wiley. (Ed. It., *Digital marketing*, Milano: Etaslibri, 2002).

Xu, Y., Goedegebuure, R., & van der Heijden, B. (2006). Customer perception, customer satisfaction, and customer loyalty within the Chinese securities business: Towards a mediation model for predicting customer behavior. *Journal of Relationship Marketing, 5*(4), 79–104.

Yim, C. K. B., Tse, D. K., & Chan, K. W. (2008). Strengthening customer loyalty through intimacy and passion: Roles of customer–firm affection and customer–staff relationships in services. *Journal of Marketing Research, 45*(6), 741–756.

Zeithaml, V. A., Berry, L. L., & Parasuraman, A. (1996). The behavioral consequences of service quality. *Journal of Marketing, 60*(April), 31–46.

Zhang, B., & He, C. (2012). Online customer loyalty improvement: Based on TAM psychological perception and loyal behavior model. *Advances in Information Technology and Management, 1*, 162–165.

CHAPTER 2

Definition and Evolution of the Variables in the Model in Marketing Studies and Research

2.1 The Evolutionary Dynamics of Markets: Factors of Change and Development of the New Business-Intensive Contexts

Nowadays, the set of business resources identifies in customer loyalty one of the most important intangible assets (Christopher, Payne & Ballantyne, 1992; Cialdini, 1984; Clemmer & Schneider, 1996; Cronin & Taylor, 1992; Crosby & Taylor, 1983; Cummings & Bromiley, 1996): as pointed out on several occasions by the management literature, loyalty is a core resource both for businesses and for customers (Darroch, 2005; Palacios Marqués & José Garrigós Simón, 2006; Smith & Rupp, 2002; Rowley, 2002; Chaudhuri & Holbrook, 2001; Hollensen, 2015; Palmatier, Jarvis, Bechkoff, & Kardes, 2009). The deep changes experienced by modern markets have progressively led businesses toward the need for a more rational analysis of their customer portfolio and turnover dynamics (Bang & Joshi, 2010; Schindehutte, Morris, & Kocak, 2008; Sirmon, Hitt, Arregle, & Campbell, 2010), concluding that the conquest of new customers can be compatible, in purely economic terms, only with high-growth markets and customers who tend to express a low churn rate (Selden & MacMillan, 2006; Tsai, 2005; Verhees, Meulenberg, & Pennings, 2010; Vrontis & Thrassou, 2007). However, the digital economy and the new evolutionary trends of markets and consumers have created a fracture with respect to the way customer loyalty was interpreted before the introduction of the Internet. Today, the acquisition of a new customer is much more expensive

M. Del Giudice, M.R. Della Peruta, *The Satisfaction of Change*,
DOI 10.1007/978-3-319-41884-1_2

than the interventions that may be implemented for retention purposes (Reichheld, 1996; Kotler, Burton, Deans, Brown & Armstrong, 2015); moreover, for this reason indeed, on the Internet, the strategic attitude of a company aims at favoring the preservation of the "capital" that is mostly at risk: loyal customers (Busacca & Castaldo, 1996, Saeidi, Sofian, Saeidi, Saeidi & Saaeidi, 2015). The warning signs of such a revolution in the concept of business, and the conditions triggering such a change in the markets, first classical (offline) and then digital (online), are numerous and varied (Shankar, Smith, & Rangaswamy, 2003; Zhang & He, 2012):

- *the growth of the information and cognitive power of customers*, supported by a process of diffusion and integration of technologies applied to the world of telecommunications. Consumers, especially for their most expensive purchases, have gradually honed their skills and needs during their shopping expeditions, giving priority to the aim of holding onto the best product/service at the most favorable terms, through more careful and conscious comparisons, consistently with a lower expenditure of time[1] (Hsieh & Li, 2008).
- *customer eclecticism* Brand loyalty has been gradually eroded in many consumer sectors by "opportunistic" behavior and a greater propensity to change (a reflection of the new patterns of consumption) (Busacca & Castaldo, 1996). The broadening and deepening of the product portfolios in many companies, the increasing number of distribution channels, the diffusion of Internet shopping, the increase in promotional activities, and the greater awareness and autonomy of customers have led to record increasing rates of disloyalty over the years (customer churn). Furthermore, while on the one hand, in the consumer market, the share of those who usually move toward a single brand has constantly diminished, on the other hand, in parallel, the proportion of those who choose within a more or less wide family of brands has increased: the final result is that for many products (such as information technology, hi-tech, and commodities in general), the final decision of a customer is more and more frequent within a range of brands, according to the most advantageous offer or the prevailing mood of the customer at the time of purchase (Busacca & Castaldo, 1996; Chen & Hu, 2010; Terrill & Middlebrooks, 2000; Dacko, 2008; Tzokas & Saren, 2004).
- *the emergence of individual and customized patterns of consumption.* The presence of a potentially unstable and heterogeneous demand

has created, more evidently than in the past, market fragmentation, leading to the birth of different lifestyles, characterized by an increasing need for personal identity and the search for high-quality and low-cost products, diversified if compared with those purchased by other consumers.[2] In such a scenario, it has therefore become vital for businesses to try to provide their customers with a strictly personalized one-to-one offer, through the establishment of stable and long-lasting relations based on mutual trust (the Web and tools provided by Internet programming have greatly encouraged firms' ability to customize offer) (Kotler, Keller, Manceau & Hémonnet-Goujot, 2015; Babin & Zikmund, 2015).

- *the search for innovation*. Closely linked to the desire of marking a distinction from the masses, a constant search for innovation and the latest "model", the most technologically advanced and evolved, is now well established in most of the customers, especially those belonging to the middle social and economic range. The result is that, today, in many industries, especially those with a high technological content (such as computers, home automation, hi-tech, and telecommunications), there is the risk of attracting new customers with the most advanced product models, but creating at the same time dissatisfaction among those who in the recent past had purchased the previous version. In many cases there is an erosion of the trust that these customers had initially placed in a company, which would therefore risk losing them[3] (East, Wright & Vanhuele, 2013; Lantos, 2015).
- *the constant rise in the expectations of consumers toward products*. Consumption patterns inspired by the search for new values have established themselves over the years: authenticity, sustainability, and durability, in addition to those relating to the performance of goods and services. In this context, once consumers have satisfied their primary basic needs, they desire that firms strive to fulfill additional needs related to them. Therefore, the customer expects to establish a full relationship with the firm, which goes beyond mere commercial transaction and allows him to solve all the problems related to a specific need: thus, nowadays, trust and customer loyalty do not pass so much only through the technical features of a product or its affordability, but mainly through the ability of a company to "be present" next to the client and to be perceived as a problem-solver (Babin & Zikmund, 2015).
- *the development of a complex and integrated offer*, where the identification of the product and service component becomes so weak

that, in many cases, a clear distinction is made impossible. Also in the past, it was very common for a product to be "enriched", for example, by support services, after-sales guarantee, etc. (the product being understood as a "basket of different attributes"). Today, this combination of products and services, and vice versa, has become a distinguishing factor of business success that firms should always keep in mind in order to fully meet the expectations of their customers, thus avoiding customers heading to more attractive offers from their competitors (Davcik & Sharma, 2015).

- *the development of the virtual market and the increasing interconnection between offer and demand.* Another trend nowadays is the increasing ability of economies to interconnect millions of people to one another with an equally large network of companies; especially through the development of the Web, the market has become more transparent and information-rich, and without space–time boundaries.[4] With these assumptions, securing loyal customers has become even more critical for businesses: in such a scenario, at the base of customer loyalty, we find the ability of a firm to meet the demands of its customers in real time, trying to promptly adapt its offer to their needs (Lovelock & Patterson, 2015).
- *market globalization and privatizations undertaken by several Western governments.* The phenomenon of globalization that is affecting most of the advanced and developing countries is forcing companies to rethink their strategic choices and their structures in the field of research, production, and marketing; the effect will be the intensification of competitive dynamics because of the greater pressure arising from international markets (Rigby & Bilodeau, 2015).

2.2 Resistance to Change, Script Theory, Post-purchase Evaluations: Literature Review of the Proposed Model

2.2.1 The Research Design and Its Conceptual Assumptions

The scale and complexity of the trends described in the previous section have required that businesses undertake a change in their strategic orientations which is sometimes radical (Le Meunier-FitzHugh & Lane, 2009; Lechner & Kreutzer, 2010; Lee, Huang, Barnes, & Kao, 2010; Lee & Kim, 2008; Masanell & Ricart, 2010; McGrath, 2010; O'Sullivan, 2010;

Pil & Holweg, 2006). Also academic research and managerial studies on demand have become increasingly aware of this since the early eighties (Deighton, 1996; Del Giudice & Del Giudice, 2003; Del Giudice & Maggioni, 2014; Del Giudice & Polski, 2003). The marketing literature has progressively based its attention on the phases of buying behavior subsequent to the initial expressions of preference for either one or the other brand/product, focusing, albeit with different approaches, on the phenomena that define the state and dynamics of the relationship between business and customer (Oliver, 1997; Doney & Cannon, 1997; Chen & Hu, 2010; Terrill & Middlebrooks, 2000; Dacko, 2008; Tzokas & Saren, 2004; Hsieh & Li, 2008; Saeidi, Sofian, Saeidi, Saeidi & Saaeidi, 2015; Kotler, Keller, Manceau & Hémonnet-Goujot, 2015; Babin & Zikmund, 2015).[5] In parallel to the now-established line of studies on consumer behavior, increasingly rich in interdisciplinary contributions, a new set of models specifically related to customer shopping behavior designed to describe and interpret it has been developed in the management literature. In particular, the theoretical considerations initially developed in the scientific literature on this topic have been rapidly applicable to the field of business. For an entrepreneur, customer centricity means, first of all, management of the interaction between the staff that is in contact with the customer and the customer himself (Grisaffe & Kumar, 1998; Hagel & Singer, 1999; Hakansson, Johanson & Wootz, 1976; Hakansson & Osteberg, 1975; Hart, Smith, Sparks & Tzokas, 1999; Hartman & Sifonis, 2000; Hax & Wilde II, 1999; Hax & Wilde II, 2001). The interest in this subject has progressively produced a considerable amount of contributions to the present day, when, in the presence of a digital economy, contact staff has been gradually replaced by a website (Ghosh, 1998). Therefore, the focus has slowly drifted toward the possible interaction between the customer and the website, between a physical and a virtual entity (Lovelock & Patterson, 2015).

The model developed in this study, despite drawing its own hypotheses on the analysis of a business-intensive context, with low supply costs and high customer disloyalty, such as the digital economy, is based on the classical theoretical assumptions of business economics, which can be essentially grouped into four areas of study (Chen & Hitt, 2000):

1. customer satisfaction;
2. the shopping experience from a customer perspective;
3. switching costs;
4. the concept of script.

The phase of literature review and theoretical conceptualization of the model is concluded by an examination of the concept of loyalty in studies on business economics, necessary to "close the loop" on the concept of "resistance to change" (Fig. 2.1).

Focusing more specifically on the marketing literature, a discipline to which this work is ascribable, it looks like the theme of the shopping experience has been often dealt mainly from a business perspective, while neglecting the customer perspective, that is, neglecting the perception that the customer has of his participation in the experience in question (Selden & MacMillan, 2006; Tsai, 2005; Vrontis & Thrassou, 2007; Ford, 1990; Gambetta, 1988). From this perception, the basic concept of this study is directly derived: the customer loyalty relationships with a firm and the perception of switching costs created by a higher level of satisfaction induced by a more complete shopping experience. In order to analyze the way the shopping experience is lived by the customer, this work uses the concept of cognitive script, which has its roots in the part of cognitive psychology that studies the organization of knowledge in the memory of individuals and turns out to be relevant and useful to describe the representation of the customer shopping experience (Abelson, 1981; Foray & Steinmueller, 2003; Schank & Abelson, 1977; Zohar & Luria, 2003). From a strictly theoretical point of view, the management literature seems to have mainly analyzed so far the implications of customer familiarity with a firm within the processes of exchange and

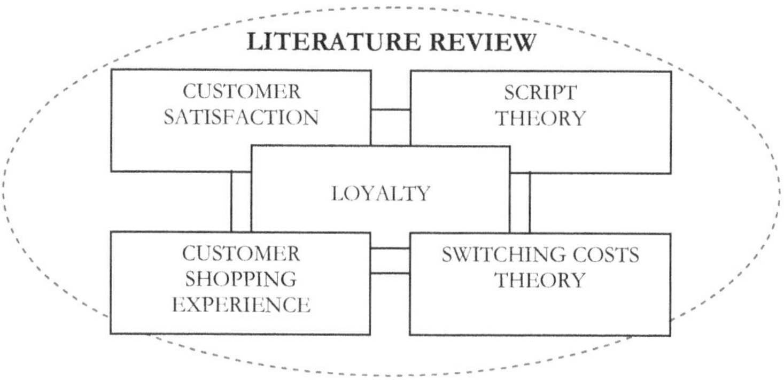

Fig. 2.1 Conceptual dimensions of the theoretical framework of the research design

consumption, highlighting the fact that a customer who knows well his relationship with the firm contributes more effectively to the management of this interaction (Bateson 1985; Farber-Canziani, 1997; Ferrata, 1997; Marion, 1996). This study, taking a cue from these contributions, has the goal of projecting in the digital economy and modern markets, dominated by ambiguity, complexity, change, and chaos, the consequences of the knowledge of the service experience (lived through the website, in this case) by the customer, on his resistance against changing supplier (Kalakota & Whinston, 1997; Kiani, 1998; Keaveney, 1995; Klemperer, 1995; Kosiur, 1997). For the purpose of a more complete understanding of the issues addressed in this study, it becomes necessary, at this stage of the discussion, to present a literature review of the lines of study on which the developed research is grounded and has inspired the model proposed.

2.2.2 *Shopping Experience, Customer Satisfaction, Resistance to Change: An Approach Path*

As it may be deduced from the above statements, the antecedents of this study can be found in the analysis of customer shopping behavior and post-purchase evaluations (Novak, Hoffman & Yung, 2000; Oliva, Oliver & MacMillan, 1992). In particular, on a great variety of complex assessments that characterize the exchange process and repurchase dynamics: economic, rational but also psychological, affective, and emotional evaluations.

From the point of view of the management literature, it should be noted that until the beginning of the eighties, most of the manuals on buying behavior[6] had given marginal attention to the post-purchase evaluation process[7]. Only in relatively recent times, the economic business literature, taking into account the profound changes in consumption patterns and, more generally, in the balance of power and the competitive dynamics of markets, has pointed out that the extension of research to post-purchase product–customer interaction and relationship marketing has to be considered vital for contemporary businesses, in order to generate new knowledge on dimensions such as customer satisfaction and customer loyalty Chandrashekaran, Rotte, Tax, & Grewal, 2007; Palmatier, Scheer, & Steenkamp, 2007; Tse, Nicosia, & Wilton, 1991; Yim, Tse, & Chan, 2008). Moreover, already at the beginning of the nineties, Iacobucci,

Grayson, and Omstrom (1992) had highlighted the lack of shared theoretical models on the issues at stake, which persisted, although the first considerable efforts to analyze the determinants of customer satisfaction and post-purchase behavior date back to the second half of the seventies (Hunt, 1977; Oliver, 1977; Olson & Dover, 1979).[8] In-depth analysis of the process of development of the relations between customers and firms, and thus the examination of post-purchase behavior, has received in the last 20 years the attention of both a part of the literature involved in the study of customer behavior, through the analysis of customer satisfaction, and another branch, which can be typically reconnected to managerial studies on relationship marketing.[9] The interest of the first scholars was initially justified by the awareness of the limited in-depth analysis of the phenomena that characterize the behavior of demand, once a preference has been expressed for a brand or a product.[10]

The focus of relationship marketing researchers, however, originated from the in-depth examination of the "social" content of certain exchange processes (Moe & Yang, 2009): especially those repeated over time (Gummesson, 1987; Hakansson & Wootz, 1979), uninterpretable and related to the classical categorization proposed by the marketing mix paradigm (Andaleeb, 1992; Ganesan, 1994; Gronroos, 1994b).[11]

However, the two lines of study can ideally represent two different moments of an in-depth analysis of a single dyadic relationship between the firm and the customer (its assumption characterizes the process of choice of a customer that repeats the purchase). From this perspective, in fact, the concept of repurchasing, a condition necessary but not sufficient for loyalty, would find in the studies on customer satisfaction the analysis on the first steps of the relationship, while those on relationship marketing would represent the final outcome of established relations (moreover, in the studies in question, the economic content of the exchange process had an almost secondary significance, probably sometimes almost ancillary, compared with its wider social weight) (Andaleeb, 1992; Chandrashekaran et al., 2007; Dwyer et al. 1987; Ganesan, 1994; Granovetter, 1985; Morgan & Hunt, 1994; Palmatier et al., 2007; Yim et al., 2008). In parallel with the managerial studies on the satisfaction in customer relationships, classical economics, and later business economics, developed a subject relating to the supposed transition from one relationship to another: the switching cost. The issue was classically examined from a twofold perspective. The first, of a psychological and organizational kind, refers to the theory of bounded rationality and its effects on the nature of transactions; the second, of a purely managerial kind, considers the different nature of switching costs and the different moments of the customer consumption experience when they may occur. At this point, it is necessary to rapidly review the theoretical contributions related to the different lines of study described, in order to give a theoretical frame to the model proposed.

This work of theoretical construction will allow the definition of the concept of "resistance to change", which is fundamental to the understanding of this study. In particular, the assumption underlying all the work is inherent in a double opportunity connected to the existence of switching costs which defend a business relationship: first, an opportunity for a firm, which has the aim of transferring to the customer some sort of shopping script, which enables a loyal relationship with the company. An opportunity for the customer (in this study, "business customer") that taking advantage of the psychological and practical benefits associated with the use of such a cognitive structure will be more reluctant to change and therefore more loyal, just because he is more satisfied.[12]

2.2.2.1 Contributions to Customer Satisfaction

The studies in question are theoretically based on the studies on personality psychology carried out by Hoppe (1930) and Lewin (1936) in the first half of the twentieth century. Investigating the construct "self-esteem/self-confidence" and its determinants, these scholars have in fact laid the conceptual and methodological bases for the development of the paradigm of "confirmation" or "disconfirmation of expectations".[13] Through the translation of the experimentation context, from personality psychology to interpersonal relations, and then to social psychology, the essence of the causal connection between satisfaction and trust toward individuals or organizations is caught (Bitner, 1995; Tähtinen & Blois, 2011).[14]

In marketing studies, the first conceptualizations on the topic (Cardozo, 1965; Hunt, 1977; Oliver, 1977, 1980; Olson & Dover, 1979) were made without explicit reference to the experimentation by Lewin's School, thus focusing research on the antecedents of satisfaction. The early pioneering studies, mainly theoretical in nature, were followed by a varied line of empirical analyses that attempted to verify or falsify the confirmation/disconfirmation paradigm (which has been in fact derived from the "discrepancy theory" developed by social psychology), producing interesting evidence with regard to intervening variables of the explanatory power of the paradigm (Fournier & Mick, 1999; Oliver, 1997; Yi, 1990).[15]

Numerous studies have revealed that the main determinant of trust is precisely satisfaction accumulated over time as a result of market transactions, the outcomes of which confirm performance expectations acquired by customers.[16] In parallel to these experimentations, since the second half of the eighties, some important managerial models have been developed (Parasuraman, Zeithaml, & Berry, 1989), and have further legitimized the result of research on customer satisfaction. Starting from the observation of the change that began to permeate all markets, these models have increasingly supported, conceptually and pragmatically, the orientation of firms toward consolidation of the relations with their customers. Finally, the latest developments of studies on customer satisfaction investigated the emotional and psychological components (Fournier & Mick, 1999; Oliver, 1997; Westbrook, 1987) of satisfaction and the evolution of the construct over time; in particular, the French school of marketing, focusing the analysis on digital contexts and the need to interpret satisfaction in terms of the perceived level of customer service, has attempted to understand the many variables involved between the perception of satisfaction, arising from the interaction with the contact staff (classic economy) or the website (digital economy), and the choice to repurchase a brand or a product (Oliver, 1999). This satisfaction, deeply inherent in the experience of the service received and the interaction lived by the customer with the company in the exchange process, is more reconnectable to loyalty if the empirical contributions on relationship marketing and service experience are more thoroughly examined (Le Meunier-FitzHugh & Lane, 2009; Lechner & Kreutzer, 2010; Lee et al., 2010; Lee & Kim, 2008; Masanell & Ricart, 2010; McGrath, 2010; O'Sullivan, 2010; Pil & Holweg, 2006).

2.2.2.2 Contributions to the Shopping Experience from a Customer Perspective

This study, as anticipated, focuses on the satisfaction arising from a positive shopping experience (the result of an effective customer service in the interaction between customer and firm). This study, as mentioned, aims at contributing to the management literature with two innovations: (a) it is an attempt to analyze the shopping experience from a customer perspective in a digital economy; (b) it is a first study of a business-to-business (B2B) market in a digital economy. In a digital economy, given the low cost of searching for alternative suppliers, the sale of a physical good is usually accompanied by a great variety of services that make buying more attractive and the relationship more loyal. In B2B markets the customer is a professional operator in the industry (Hutt & Speh, 2012), therefore, its purchase takes into account the technical aspects of the product (since it often already has previous knowledge of the product it intends to buy), the price (since the purchase is intended for resale to the end user), but above all, the services offered by the website (in the case of an online purchase), which come along with the product. Thus, it is plausible to consider the interaction between the operator of a B2B market and its online supplier as a concept closely relatable to the one of service encounter.[17] The concept has its roots in a vast and heterogeneous literature. At the beginning of the eighties, Grönroos (1983) spoke for the first time of "interactive" marketing, with the aim of defining the relevance of the interaction between customer and supplier. The scholar stated that the quality perceived by the customer and his repurchasing behavior were strictly dependent on the (perceived) quality of interaction, or the fact that the attention given to the style in which service is provided in the sales process is equal to the care for the result. During the same period, Berry (1983) coined the term "relationship marketing".[18] Starting from the empirical evidence found in B2B markets, some northern European authors have begun to investigate the features of the exchange processes repeated over time and based on social, dyadic, and network relationships that promote cooperative behavior and real partnerships between sellers and buyers.[19] Stable relationships between customers and suppliers, defined in a broad sense, have been studied in many contexts in later years. In particular, attempting a brief systematization of the contributions to the literature, it is possible to identify the following fields of investigation:

- *distribution channels* (Andaleeb, 1992; Anderson & Narus, 1990; Anderson & Weitz, 1989; Castaldo, 1994; Shurr & Ozanne, 1985);
- *consumer markets* (Fletcher & Peters, 1997; Gurviez, 1996);
- *services* (Crosby, Evans, & Cowles, 1990; Grayson & Ambler, 1999; Moorman, Deshpandé, & Zaltman, 1993; Moorman, Zaltman, & Deshpandé, 1992).

Starting from a fundamental contribution by Dwyer et al. (1987), the most important studies on relationship marketing have highlighted the central role of trust in purchase repetition (in this contribution, researchers identified it as a key factor for the transition from discrete market transactions to continuous exchange relations). Right from the researches in the mid-eighties, trust was considered one of the crucial determinants of stable and cooperative relationships[20] (Andersen & Kumar, 2006; Tähtinen & Blois, 2011). Later, within in-depth analyses on market relations, different conceptualizations were suggested, both one-dimensional and multi-dimensional, with respect to which, however, there are controversial and often heterogeneous positions.[21] The only element not arising any doubt is related to the cognitive dimension of trust defined by the predictability of the counterpart's behavior, namely the perception of reliability based on experience, and more specifically on a sequence of transactions/interactions characterized by the confirmation of performance and satisfaction expectations (Oliver, 1997).

In addition to trust, the studies on relationship marketing have highlighted other constructs that characterize the most stable and long-lasting relationships. Among others, subjects of specific research and experimentation have been: commitment,[22] stability, interaction, power, influence, dependency, reciprocity, and cooperation[23] (Berry & Parasuraman, 1991; Bucklin & Sengupta, 1993; Sterne & El Ansary, 1992; Tunisini, 1999). Gruen (1995), in particular, linked the concept of relational commitment and satisfaction, arising from fairness perceived in the exchange process, to opportunistic behavior, assuming that a high perception of fairness and consolidated commitment in the relationship significantly reduces the risk of opportunistic behavior. Finally, also as part of the studies on relationship marketing, the first models of life cycle of a relationship were proposed in the eighties. Several authors, in fact, argued that, while the empirical evidence of the relationship constructs and their determinants and consequences are based on the state of the relationship at a given point in time, it is plausible to assume that there are no real paths of development in relationships. Among the various models proposed, one of the best known is that of Ford (1980, 1998), which identifies five stages (later reduced to four) of development of a relationship. Similarly, Dwyer, Schurr, and Oh (1987) suggest a model of life cycle of a relationship divided in five stages: awareness, exploration, expansion, commitment, and dissolution.

The main difference with Ford's model is to be found in the dissolution of the relationship, which according to the authors is characterized by unilateral decisions, unlike the other phases that require a typically synchronic reciprocity of attitudes and behavior.[24] Some authors propose some interesting experimental evidence of the behavior that characterizes the evolutionary process of a relationship and, in particular, the role of networks of relationships that the actors of a given dyad are able to activate. (Bion, 2013; Gersick, 1988; Yalom & Leszcz, 2005).[25] Studies on relationship marketing, mainly thanks to the extensive application of theories borrowed from social psychology and analytical and conceptual tools of sociological nature, are one of the most prolific lines of study in the field of managerial disciplines. Many theoretical models and empirical evidence have been developed in the last two decades regarding the nature, determinants, and consequences of market relationships. Certainly, the diffusion of online shopping has profoundly altered the relationships between market players, laying the foundations for a renewed vision of relationship marketing (Le Meunier-FitzHugh & Lane, 2009; Lechner & Kreutzer, 2010; Lee et al., 2010; Lee & Kim, 2008; Masanell & Ricart, 2010; McGrath, 2010).

2.2.2.3 Contributions to the Switching Costs Theory

After outlining the features of a literature review of "customer satisfaction" and "shopping experience" constructs, it is now time to consider the studies on the customer's decision-making process, facing the option to buy or not from the same supplier (Keaveney, 1995; Klemperer, 1995; Kosiur, 1997). In managerial studies, the so-called "resistance to change" is the explanation of the so-called switching costs (Meng & Elliott, 2009). In the study of individual decision-making processes, a fundamental contribution to an understanding of how individuals manage this process has been provided by the theory of bounded rationality, starting from Simon's research (1977). The theory of bounded rationality is an answer to the theories of choice that consider an individual as a perfectly rational decision-maker, capable of evaluating with precision the moment of choice, the range of available alternatives, and the consequences that may result from each choice. The observation of how the decision-making process does not take place under conditions of perfect information regarding the available alternatives and the consequences that may result from each alternative, but rather in terms of uncertainty about the future consequences (in other words, individuals, as decision-makers, would only know the probabilities of the various possible outcomes in relation to their actions). Moreover, March (1994) states that individuals, during the decision-making process, are bound by a limited cognitive ability and by the impossibility of obtaining complete information about the possible consequences of their different actions. The cognitive constraints, as understood by the scholar, essentially appear as informational constraints[26]; in the presence of these constraints and, more generally, of the phenomenon of bounded rationality, individuals activate certain processes of decision simplification (Kahneman & Tversky, 1973; Nisbett & Ross,

1980). Therefore, bounded rationality appears as a source of a number of semantic distortions in an individual's decision-making process. In the phase of information search and assessment of alternatives, for example, the cost and difficulty of the search process can lead individuals to be willing, in an often spontaneous and unconscious manner, to limit research by moving in familiar and well-known directions.[27]

The theory of bounded rationality has not only been used to understand the decision-making process of individuals and the presence of switching costs. Coase (1937), for example, states that the space for business development arises from the existence of limits to the capacity of information processing by the actors involved in the decision-making process, and therefore, generally, from the existence of costs of information collection, decision-making, negotiation, and control. Williamson (1975), developing Coase's theories, places at the center of his analysis the transactions in goods and services between businesses, noting that each transaction with the market implies some costs (Williamson, 1975), and their level is influenced by three conditions: specificity, uncertainty, and frequency of the transaction. Williamson's model of transaction costs was the starting point for further considerations in the literature. Barney and Ouchi (1984) extended and generalized Williamson's typology, recognizing other mechanisms for transaction management. More precisely, the authors identify situations in which, together with forms of regulation of pure market transactions, there are also intermediate situations implemented both through the use of explicit rules and procedures, and through collaboration and reciprocity relationships (defined as "clan relationships"). According to the intensity of two features of a transaction, the ambiguity in performance assessment and the expected longevity, Barney and Ouchi (1984) identify different mechanisms of transaction management: an internal government with the features of a clan, while average levels recommend an external clan relationship. Pure market situations are proposed in situations of low ambiguity and low longevity. In line with what Williamson (1975) stated, transaction conditions (specificity, uncertainty, and frequency) influence the customer's choice of an ongoing and privileged relationship with a single supplier. For example, with regard to specificity, one could think of the mutual knowledge that can develop between a customer and a supplier who cooperate continuously (which is even more true in the case of B2B): knowledge of languages, purchase preferences, administrative procedures, the quality of results, etc. The activities carried out are in fact specific idiosyncratic resources of that relationship. Moreover, and this helps even more to understand the links between this theory and the switching costs, with reference to uncertainty, several authors in the literature (Murray, 1991; Zeithaml, 1981; Zeithaml & Bitner, 1996) argue that the intangible nature of the service and the inseparability between production and consumption make it particularly difficult to evaluate the characteristics of a service. Consequently, in the presence of such informational complexity, the cost of establishing new transactions in addition to those already known may be too high and suggest investing in a collaborative relationship with the current supplier (which is even more true if the collaborative relationship identifies as its assumption the overall customer satisfaction in the established relationship). At this point in the discussion, it is worth recalling the contributions developed in economics, business strategy, and marketing with regard to the concept of switching costs. In economics, for example, Klemperer (1987a) postulates the existence of three types of switching costs: transaction costs (which occur during the opening and termination of a relationship), learning costs (costs that an individual or a company have to incur in order to learn to use a new product or service), and contract costs (mainly generated by a firm with the dual aim of rewarding loyal customers and retaining new ones). In strategy, in studies in the field of industrial goods, Porter (1986, p. 10) defines switching costs as "one-time costs that a buyer has to incur when changing from a product supplier to another". The author identifies four types of costs: costs associated with changing a product to adapt to the products of the new supplier, the investment required to train staff, investment in additional equipment necessary to use the products of the new supplier, and the psychological costs related to the termination of the relationship. From a more general perspective, Jackson (1985) states that switching costs are related to the effort in terms of time and money that the industrial customer must make to adapt to new products and systems of the supplier. But although the creation of switching costs in the relationship is a strategy commonly used to increase loyalty in industrial markets, the concept has been also addressed in the context of marketing. Guiltinan (1989), for example, argues that switching costs are a mechanism that can be used to develop continuous relationships with the customer. Dick and Basu (1994), in turn, argue that switching costs can result in the choice settings of end consumers. Furthermore, Fornell (1992, p. 11) states that "all financial, psychological, learning costs, etc. associated with the abandonment of a supplier for another are switching costs".

The types of switching costs to which this study refers are those developed by Klemperer (1987a), Guiltinan (1989), and Gremler (1995), and were recently analyzed in detail by Jones, Mothersbaugh, and Beatty (2002): continuity costs, learning costs, and sunk costs. A definition of continuity costs was first proposed by Guiltinan (1989) on the grounds that the specific expertise and skills acquired by a supplier in fully satisfying customer expectations may be a measure of deterrence to change suppliers (Jones et al., 2002, pp. 442–443, identify in this category the so-called lost performance costs).[28] These costs include in their definition also the risk perceived by a customer in replacing a known service with another, as the probability of it being at the same level is low and the consequences in case of failure can be severe (Jones et al., 2002, p. 443, identify in this category the so-called uncertainty costs).[29] Therefore, a customer may familiarize with the rules and procedures of a supplier to the extent he will absolutely not take into account changing to another supplier, fearing that the new one could be very different from the one he is used to (Krumske, 1987, quoted by Gremler, 1995).[30] Otherwise, learning costs represent the costs required to learn how to use a new product or service (Klemperer, 1987a, 1987b).[31] In other words, when a customer has some experience regarding transactions with his supplier, he accumulates a series of specific skills which are "non transferable, and make other [suppliers] seem less attractive and, therefore, reduce the urge to change, even if the search does not cost anything" (Klemperer, 1987a). The economic literature mentions several times the need, for a client who decides to change his usual supplier, to accumulate a series of "novice user skills" (Farrell & Shapiro, 1988; Krumske, 1987; Wernerfelt, 1985). These skills or "customer know-how" (Soellner, 1994) represent the knowledge of their role within the modalities of the exchange relationship. Thus, changing supplier would require an investment in terms of time and effort to learn a new process. In this view, brand loyalty comes from a progressive adaptation during which the customer learns to use better the features of the supply system, and then to maximize the value of the established relationship (Holbrook, 1999; Houston, 1986; Howard, 1977; Jaworski & Kohli, 1993; Johnson, 1982; Jones, Motherbaugh & Beatty, 2000; Jones & Sasser, 1992). For the author, the result of this mutual adaptation is the basis of resistance to change toward apparently more comfortable alternatives (Lund, 1985; Maccallum & Harrison, 1985). In this regard, Heskett, Sasser, and Hart (1990, p. 44) justify the customer's tendency to continue the relationship with his usual supplier with the "natural aversion to learn new routines linked to the service". In the literature, Jones et al. (2002, p. 443) suggested to distinguish learning costs in evaluation and pre-switching costs,[32] cognitive or behavioral post-switching costs,[33] and finally setup costs[34] (this study is also based on this distinction).[35]

In the end, the costs of depreciation or "psychological involvement" (sunk costs) are attributable to the expenses a customer has incurred in the past and that, despite having a greater impact in the present state, continue to be psychologically relevant. Dick and Basu (1994, p. 2) emphasize the psychological and unreal nature of these costs, stating that they "are not relevant, since it is the trade-off between current and future costs (and not those incurred in the past) that should determine expectations in terms of utility by a rational customer and then act on the decision-making process". Thus, the existence of these costs is reduced to a psychological component that concerns the level of not only money but also time and energy spent by the customer to learn how to use a product or a service, a definition that is similar to the concept of learning cost previously examined. The authors demonstrate that sunk costs have a significant impact on customer loyalty, both in terms of attitude and behavior. The studies of Jones et al. (2002) have greatly inspired a part of this study. From the analysis of the literature, not only a substantial individual difficulty emerges in analyzing the new information coming from the environment, but also a tendency not to change the patterns previously acquired and to use methods of decision which tend to confirm previous purchasing behavior. Thus, the maintenance of the relationship with a single supplier allows, on the one hand, to eliminate start-up costs of new transactions and, on the other, to benefit from the advantages arising from the longevity of the relationship, such as the creation of a common language between supplier and customer, the reduction of uncertainty about the final outcome of the performance, the moderation of opportunistic behavior, and serial fairness in the relationship (Chaarlas, Rajkumar, Kogila, Lydia, & Noorunisha, 2012). Translating this theory to the online shopping experience of a business customer, some initial interesting conclusions emerge, which are fundamental to the development of the research design of this study. It is plausible, for instance, to assume that the repetition of an operation (such as surfing through certain search tools or simplified paths within a website to complete a shopping expedition) and the acquisition of a behavioral script (explaining knowledge of that particular type of path that conducts to purchase) lead customers to recall the known script at the time of buying and repeat purchase from the same company, using as a rule in their decision-making process the repetition of a familiar and well-known situation (Hoffman, Novak & Chatterjee, 1995; Hoffman & Novak, 1996), especially if the known situation was a bearer of satisfaction. In this view, the present study does not stop to say that a business customer limits his purchasing choice based on the mere availability of the script in his memory, as stated by part of the cognitive psychology literature (see Abelson (1976), according to whom, "the mere participation in a script increases the likelihood of future participation, even if the outcome of the situation does not provide an explicit reward", p. 45; see also Nisbett & Ross, 1980). However, going further, it attempts to prove, with the support of the empirical analysis discussed in detail in Chap. 4, how, in a context such as the digital economy characterized by a highly competitive dynamism, a script based on the deep satisfaction experienced by an individual who lived in it determines a greater probability that the same script will be reused, just because the cost of losing the script would be excessive in the individual's perception (Bruggen, Foubert, & Gremler, 2011; Hsu & Chiang, 2011; Jacobs & De Klerk, 2010).[36]

2.2.2.4 Contributions to the Script Theory

In cognitive psychology the script is a variant of the frame introduced by Roger Schank in 1977, a memory structure that represents stereotypical knowledge related to sequences of actions. Scripts originate from a social phenomenon, knowledge sharing of stereotypical actions with other human beings. This social phenomenon, in turn, is exploited by the mind to simplify reasoning in all situations that are part of it. In each of those situations, the mind does not need to perform complex logical reasoning that would be theoretically required, but simply runs the corresponding script[37] (Schank & Abelson, 1977; Woofford, 1994). The script belongs to the larger family of cognitive schemas, a concept studied in cognitive psychology at the beginning of the thirties (Barlett, 1932, was one of the first scholars to take an interest in the concept). It is, in particular, a schema that contains the knowledge of the timeline of an event (Engel et al., 1968).[38] The script theory argues for the need and importance of repeating acquired patterns. As noted, moreover, in a research by Tansik and Smith (1991), the repetition of stereotypical actions allows the script to become a customary behavior. This script is used to understand the event itself by an individual to reduce his cognitive effort (Woofford, 1994).[39]

The progress made over the years by cognitive psychology (Fisk & Taylor, 1991) has aroused a growing interest of various scholars in business issues, committed to verify the applicability of the concept of script to their research.[40] Instrumental to the model developed in this study is the examination of the research on the applicability of the concept of script to the relationship between seller and customer. A part of the literature has focused in particular on the seller's behavior (Leigh & McGraw, 1989; Meng Leong, Busch, & Roedder, 1989; Shurr, 1986).

The application of the script to the relationship in question starts from the basic consideration that sellers develop, in the course of their experience, knowledge of a number of procedures suitable to each situation of sale (Leigh & McGraw, 1989); in fact, to be effective, sellers need a very elaborate kind of knowledge that enables them to identify the type of sale, classify the type of customer, and select the most appropriate sales and retention strategies (Meng Leong et al., 1989). Through experience, these strategies are transformed into a series of behavioral scripts. In an entirely specular way, another branch of the literature has analyzed the buyer's behavior using the concept of script and demonstrating that buyers develop, in the course of several interactions with the sales structure, a number of stereotyped actions arranged in sequence (Leigh & Rethans, 1983; Stoltman, Tapp, & Lapidus, 1989).

According to these authors, these actions are scripts that guide the buyer's thoughts, allow him to develop a set of expectations, and behave in an appropriate manner during the shopping expedition. In a first work, Leigh and Rethans (1983) focused more on the methodological issues related to the evocation of the script; in fact, the authors demonstrated that the number and level of detail of the actions evoked are influenced both by the mode of elicitation, and by whether or not the seller's role is included in the script. In a later work, the authors were interested in the script of industrial buyers, proving once again that the evocation of the script is an alternative methodology for the identification of the phases in the shopping process of this type of buyer. Also the later study by Stoltman et al. (1989) confirms, moreover, the sequential and homogeneous structure of the script. The study is focused on the customers who go to different points of sale (typically disloyal), and in this sense, the results of the study confirm and extend the role played by the context for the activation of the script (some sequences are repeated, others seem to be firm specific) (Bozinoff & Roth, 1983; Nottenburg & Shoben, 1980). Moreover, the concept of "expectation" underlying the execution of a shopping script is also the basis of the studies on customer satisfaction through the disconfirmation paradigm (Oliver, 1980) and the extent of the gap between expectations and final result (Anderson, 1973; Oliver, 1980; Swan & Trawick, 1981; Tse & Wilson, 1988). In a similar way, and this point can be considered as an important assumption in this study, Alford (1998) shows that not only a negative deviation from the script influences satisfaction and intention to repeat purchase (automatically implying resistance to change in case of satisfactory confirmation of the script), but also a positive deviation from the script, intended as a pleasant but unexpected action, has a positive effect on the overall level of satisfaction and intention to repurchase.

From a managerial point of view (Iederan, Curseu, Vermeulen, & Geurts, 2011), these studies allow to reflect on the concept of customer satisfaction in terms of coherence between the learned and due script, and the firm's offer, both in terms of process and result. The assumption on which this study is based is very similar, moreover, to the hypotheses developed by Hubbert et al. in 1995, with regard to the coincidence between the script learned by the customer and the one transferred by the supplier. The interaction between the actors in the course of a performance can verify the existence of idiosyncratic relations between them. In this case of coincidence between the induced script and the learned script, the authors identify the potential satisfaction and speculate on the customer's resistance to change, even though they do not verify it (Hubbert, Garcia Sehorn, & Brown, 1995). This concept introduces the theme, latent throughout this study, of the opportunity a customer has of changing the shopping script. The literature on cognitive schemas has pointed out that the benefits of using a scheme are related to the reduction of the cognitive effort in executing the activities contained in the script and the ease of processing new information. These benefits, combined with the tendency of individuals to maintain their convictions unaltered and consolidate the existing schema, create indeed resistance to change. Thus, changing schemas is cognitively costly, and time-consuming, and it requires the elaboration of information and the subversion of what has been built. If in the acquired schema customer satisfaction is inherent, as the script allows a pleasant, fruitful, and rapid shopping expedition, then the resistance to change will be even stronger, and it will be possible to view switching costs in a "positive" light. The important managerial consequence arising from this discussion is the ability to retain a customer on the basis of psychological and cognitive costs that would be necessary to incur in order to change the learned shopping script, if such script is a bearer of customer satisfaction.

2.3 An Examination of the Concept of Loyalty

The examined dimensions are binding elements for the definition of the proposed model of customer retention. The varied attention given to the subject by the marketing literature, but more in general by the management literature, explains the presence of numerous and heterogeneous contributions to the analysis and understanding of customer behavior and its perceptions (Chandrashekaran et al., 2007; Palmatier et al., 2007; Yim et al., 2008). At this level of discussion, it is useful to conclude the phase of literature review by examining the contributions on loyalty, since resistance to change and simultaneous satisfaction, which are constructs examined in the previous sections, are their most direct antecedents. The analysis perspective is confirmed by numerous studies: the first works began at a time when the competitive dynamics of markets appeared very static. In particular, the first work on loyalty is attributable to Copeland (1923),[41] followed by the contributions of many other authors (to the point that in 1978, Jacoby and Chestnut could collect over 300 articles and no less than 53 definitions of loyalty). The seminar work of Jacoby (1971), Newman and Werbel (1973), and Jacoby and Kyner (1973), resumed by the well-known contribution by Jacoby and Chestnut (1978), highlighted the fundamental distinction between behavioral loyalty and mental loyalty, clarifying that repurchasing behavior is not sufficient evidence of customer loyalty.[42] The management literature has generally expressed a unanimous view, considering loyalty as a nonrandom repurchasing behavior (behavioral loyalty) of a brand/product or a group of brands/products, as a result of a particular evaluation process (mental loyalty).[43] Thus, empirical studies in the literature identify different forms of loyalty, defining repurchasing behavior not supported by a corresponding mental loyalty as "inertial purchasing" phenomena.[44] On the basis of these early works, studies on loyalty have focused on two main phenomena:

- loyalty behavior to one or more brands, characterized by variable degrees of substitutability/complementarity, and examination of the problems related to the structural measurement of loyalty and disloyal behavior (*switching behavior*)[45];
- mental/cognitive loyalty and therefore the perceptions, attitudes, and beliefs that may determine the different forms of loyalty.

The first area of research has produced several models able to measure the intensity of repurchase behavior, that is, behavioral loyalty. In particular, several structural indicators have been suggested (relating, for example, to the percentage of purchases, their sequence, the probabilities of purchase/repurchase by the customer, etc.) to be useful to measure the phenomenon analytically (and to understand the concept of shopping script, the crucial point of this study). Nevertheless, all studies on behavioral loyalty, however in-depth and rigorous in methodological terms, have a basic limitation relatively to the inability to detect only with structural measures the actual state of customer relationships (moreover, for this reason indeed, structural measures must be complemented with indicators derived from the study of the cognitive dimension of loyalty). With reference to the second area of study, instead, some models have been developed, relating to both the measurement of the sole cognitive dimension[46] and the combined measurement of cognitive and behavioral dimensions. Among the various models proposed, the contributions by Wind (1977), Dick and Basu (1994), and Busacca and Castaldo (1996) are to be highlighted as they allow to consider both dimensions. Wind (1977), in particular, proposed to classify the different forms of loyalty crossing the cognitive dimension, expressed by the level of customer satisfaction toward a certain brand, and the behavioral dimension, measured by the rate of repurchase of the same brand (Fig. 2.2).

Studies by Dick and Basu (1994), following a similar path of study, proposed to measure the cognitive dimension of loyalty in terms of relative

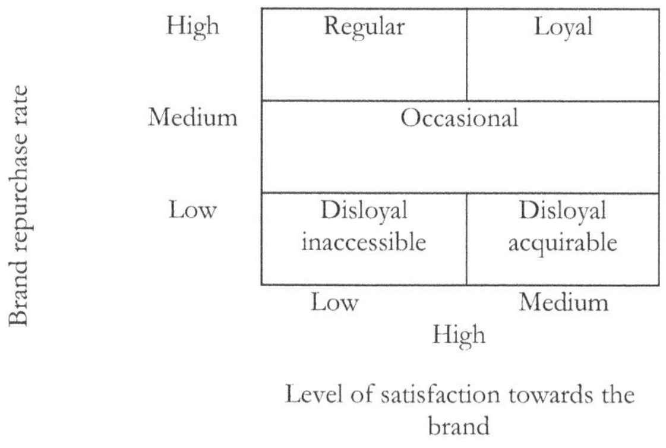

Fig. 2.2. Types of customer loyalty (Wind, 1977)

attitude, that is, assessment expressed by a customer with reference to the superiority/inferiority of the brand purchased more frequently (*focal brand*) than the alternative offers considered (Fig. 2.3).

At the extremes, relative positive evaluation and high purchasing repetition, and negative evaluation and low repetition, respectively, quadrants 2 and 4 of the matrix, are the forms of *true loyalty*[47] (to use Jacoby and Chestnut's words) and disloyalty. In quadrants 1 and 3, instead, it is possible to observe:

- forms of latent loyalty, understood as a combination of high mental loyalty not matched by an equally high behavioral loyalty to a focal brand[48];
- forms of spurious loyalty, which are forms of loyalty not supported by clear causal links, such as those found among preference toward the brand, satisfaction arising from purchasing it, trust in the brand and company, and hence involvement in the selection and intention of repurchasing it.[49]

Recently, the classification of the different forms of loyalty in relation to the two dimensions of mind and behavior was explained by Busacca and Castaldo (1996). In their research, the authors crossed four types of loyalty (full, hopeful, unstable, and distrust) with different levels of intensity of repurchasing the brand or sign (null, low, medium, and high), creating a matrix characterized by 16 different types of loyalty.[50] Among the authors who have devoted more attention to loyalty in a dynamic view, there is definitely Oliver (1999), who identifies four different phases in

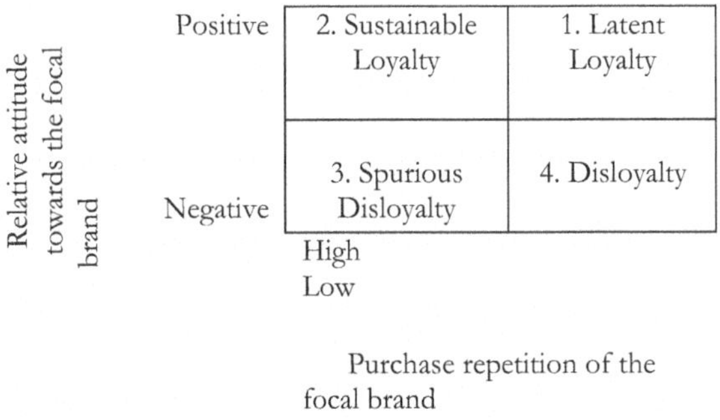

Fig. 2.3 A classification of the types of loyalty (Dick & Basu, 1994)

the relationship that develops between a customer and a firm, from the moment the customer expresses a mental preference for the firm to the moment the customer translates his ideas into action, giving rise to the actual repurchase.[51]

Only recently, the importance of the dual characterization of loyalty has become prominent in managerial studies; in fact, in previous contributions, it was customary to associate loyalty only to the behavioral aspect, that is, repeated purchasing behavior toward the same offer (firm or product/service). In relation to this dimension, loyalty materializes when a customer, in order to meet a particular need, turns unequivocally and repeatedly to the same brand/firm. But then, recent studies (Iasevoli, 2000) have shown that, although the link between repetitive behavior and customer loyalty is clear, the former is a necessary but not sufficient condition for the concrete manifestation of the latter; in fact, with the sole behavioral dimension, a repetitive buying behavior appears, which is lacking in motivation and may be susceptible to change as a result of actions taken by competitors (Fig. 2.4).

In fact, from the analysis of the four quadrants of the matrix of customer loyalty proposed by Iasevoli (2000), it results that:

- *absolute loyalty* is achieved in the presence of an extremely positive attitude toward the firm's offer associated with buying behavior exclusively oriented to the range of the firm's products/services;
- *induced loyalty* is determined not only by an exclusive buying behavior but also by a negative attitude toward the firm's offer. In this case, loyalty can be induced by a variety of factors, among which the most frequent concern, for example, a scarce presence of competing

Fig. 2.4 The matrix of customer loyalty (Iasevoli, 2000)

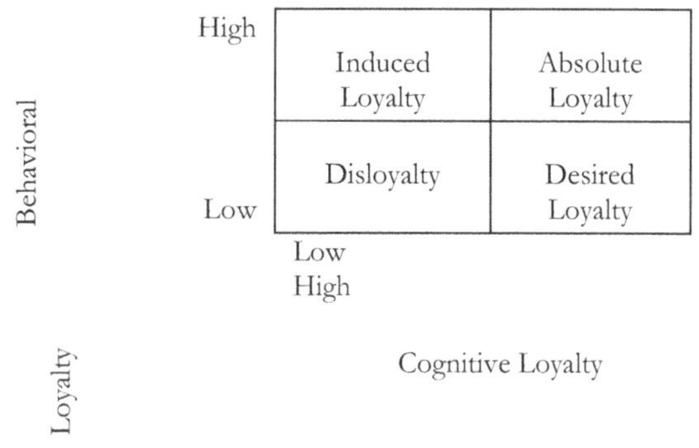

products, high reconversion costs, which can be economic, of use (costs of learning the new offer), or time (the narrow margins of time to choose new suppliers) or affect the presence of exit barriers, etc. Of course, such a situation is very risky for an enterprise because the customer could move toward its competitors as restraining factors decrease;

Repurchase rate of the brand or sign / Intensity of trust in the brand or sign	High	Medium (hopeful)	Low	Null
High	Consumers loyal to the brand/sign	Regular and hopeful consumers of the brand/sign	Regular but unstable consumers of the brand/sign	Regular but discouraged consumers of the brand/sign
Medium	Occasional but confident consumers of the brand/sign	Occasional but hopeful consumers of the brand/sign	Occasional but unstable consumers of the brand/sign	Occasional but discouraged consumers of the brand/sign
Low	Random but confident consumers of the brand/sign	Random but hopeful consumers of the brand/sign	Random but unstable consumers of the brand/sign	Random but discouraged consumers of the brand/sign
Null	Consumers of other brands that trust the brand/sign	Consumers of other brands hopeful towards the brand/sign	Consumers of other brands with unstable trust in the brand/sign	Segment of demand inaccessible to the brand/sign

Fig. 2.5 A schema for the identification of customers loyal to a certain brand or sign (Busacca & Castaldo, 1996)

- *desired loyalty* occurs when a customer, while expressing a positive attitude toward the firm's offer turns to the products of competitors. The situation can be justified by the presence of restraining factors that could affect the competing products and prevent the customer to direct his choices to the offer that is closest to his needs;
- *disloyalty* occurs when the customer turns to the offer of competitors because his perception of the latter is significantly better than that of the firm that is conducting the analysis.

Busacca and Castaldo (1996) identified instead 16 situations of loyalty arising from crossing the different types of loyalty proposed by Andaleeb (1992) and the different levels relating to the rate of repurchase of the brand/sign proposed by Wind (1977); the extremes are represented by consumers actually inaccessible by a given brand/sign and loyal consumers, as regular buyers characterized by full and stable trust (reliability, perception of a firm's high capacity of nonopportunism) (Fig. 2.5). Therefore, only the buyers classified in the upper left quadrant can be considered loyal as the transient nature of the preferences of the other consumer groups is clear. In particular, regular but discouraged buyers constitute a highly risky segment, still bound to the firm for the existence of barriers to exit from the relationship, for the lack of alternatives or the substantial indifferentiation among them, but certainly ready, as these constraints ease off, to abandon it.

Notes

1. This trend has been greatly facilitated by the development of the Web in recent years and the gradual increase in users' surfing speed. Nowadays, this is made possible by the progressive reduction in the acquisition prices of Internet technologies, even for home users (this is the case of the diffusion of the broadband and DSL [digital subscriber line] technologies). The higher surfing speed and the increasingly massive diffusion of comparative portals, offering the possibility to find on the Web the prices of thousands of items sold online by different e-retailers and to compare them, have raised the cognitive power of customers to unprecedented levels (see www.kelkoo.it).
2. These observations are the basis of what is now commonly referred to as differential marketing. The same assumptions have created over the years the conditions for a kind of "self-segmentating" demand, and a classic example is to be found in tribe marketing studies.
3. In the mentioned industries, in fact, the risk of product cannibalization is very high as it is triggered by obsolescence, induced, in turn, precisely by the need for innovation in demand.

4. Today, in fact, the reference is to no-space management as the possibility offered by the Web to activate and complete transactions without constraints of time or space, by simply operating online (Moe & Yang, 2009).
5. During the nineties, the importance of customer relationships emerging in hypercompetitive environments interested the academic community, which developed the new line of post-consumption research, and had obvious repercussions on business investments in marketing research. According to some estimates reported by Oliver (1999), in those years, the budget allocated to customer research (customer satisfaction, etc.) far exceeded 30 % of the total amount invested by companies in marketing research.
6. In this regard, see the classics by Howard (1963), Nicosia (1966), Engel, Kollat, and Blackwell (1968), and Howard and Sheth (1969), up to the latest editions of the volumes by Assael (1995), and Peter and Olson (1996).
7. In these studies there is no detail regarding the varied dynamics of the customer's buying behavior, during the life cycle of his relationship with the company, but a mere description of the plethora of post-purchase evaluations as a set of perceptions from which the feedback flow on the motivational and perceptual systems stems, returning the feedback process exclusively to the basis of the "satisfaction–dissatisfaction" dyad (Ball, Coelho, & Machás, 2004; Gijsbrechts, Heerde, & Pauwels, 2008; Van Heerde & Bijmolt, 2005).
8. Moreover, during the eighties (and in all the following decades), the experiments and managerial applications were numerous and varied in this respect. For a useful comparison, see the studies by Oliver (1980, 1981), Churchill and Suprenant (1982), Tse and Wilton (1988), Fournier and Mick (1999).
9. It should be pointed out that studies on relationship marketing have adopted as a unit of investigation the "relationship" defined in a broad sense. In fact, the majority of the work, both conceptual and empirical, produced by this line of study examined the network of business relationships and their influence on trade, starting from industrial goods and progressively extending the range of analysis to all business-to-business (B2B) markets. Thus, the analysis perspective was sometimes that of the "buyer–seller" dyad (basic unit of investigation), sometimes the network of relationships activated by buyers and sellers; finally, at other times, the relationship dynamics that alternate exchanges within a dyad, with evaluations and comparisons, and possible exchange processes, which involve a more or less wide network of relationships, were taken into account.
10. On the subject, several empirical contributions produced between the late eighties and the nineties were decisive. See, among others, Ford (1980), Day and Wensley (1983), Dwyer, Schurr, and Oh (1987), Gronroos (1994a, 1994b), and Webster (1994a, 1994b).
11. These authors trace back to the contributions by Kotler and Levy (1969), and those by Bagozzi (1974, 1975), the first considerations on the revision

of the concept of exchange exclusively based on the economic dimensions of a transaction. Thus, at the end of the sixties, the explanatory extent of marketing paradigms probably began to expand in the direction of the conceptualization of exchange and market relationships, which were not only economic.

12. The developed model, according to the current research settings of the French school of marketing, seeks to explore the opportunity of creating barriers, positively perceived by a customer when he breaks the relationship. A way of remaining loyal not because he is somehow "forced" to do so (→ for lack of opportunities to change or excessive onerosity), but because he "wants" to do so (→ perception of serial fairness in the relationship and extreme satisfaction). Therefore, the study considers the experience of shopping online from the customer's point of view (unlike many studies in the literature that take into account the shopping experience only from the company's perspective). The basic hypothesis is that there is an online shopping script, different from one website to another, consisting of a behavioral base (which we would call "inertial") and a cognitive base (which we would call "spontaneous"). Satisfaction inherent in the script, as a result of the positive perception of the shopping expedition, creates a special lock-in mechanism in the customer, a "positive" retention (in contrast to the classical school of economics that viewed the lock-in as a subtle strategy of loyalization, mainly based on the fact that the customer does not change supplier because switching would cost too much, *regardless* of its degree of satisfaction (Shapiro & Varian, 1999)). In the present study, the customer does not switch because changing would cost him too much in terms of satisfaction, because he would essentially lose the acquired shopping script, which allows him to operate in an optimal way. Another innovation suggested by this study is the analysis of a B2B digital market (differently from almost all of the empirical evidence, based on business-to-customer [B2C] markets).
13. The relationship between confidence and self esteem, as it is currently known in the studies on social psychology, does not seem to be due only to the commonality of the "trust" construct. In fact, it can be imagined that repeated experiences of confirmation of expectations end up increasing, indeed, the certainty that individuals acquire about their ability to evaluate and select an alternative offer (Bandura, 1982, 1986). This relationship, which is studied both in the context of personality psychology and social psychology, may explain some of the processes of self-gratification generated by customer satisfaction.
14. In this regard, it should be noted that trust has often been defined as "conviction" or "belief". However, complying precisely with the one-dimensional definition of the trust construct—that still appears to be the only one to have passed all the numerous attempts of falsification, conducted by the

proposition, operationalization, and testing of alternative definitions (Blois, 1999; Raymond, 1999)—rather than a belief, it seems to be an attitude, defined as the predisposition learned—hence the result of experience—to respond in a certain way to a particular object (Fishbein & Ajzen, 1975). Trust, in fact, would be a prejudice, generated by a sequence of acknowledgments or disconfirmations of expectations of behavior (performance) that, in the form of extreme rationality, translates into a probability assigned to the occurrence of a given behavior (performance) of a defined counterparty (a company). Belief, however, would imply certainty, not always based on fully rational evaluations (faith or "trust"). In this regard, a great interest arises from the distinctions between faith, trust, and "confidence", suggested by Hart (1989) and Luhman (1989). An alternative distinction between attitude and belief was suggested by Oliver (1997), according to whom, belief expresses an informative condition typical of the cognitive sphere—hence, for example, the probability, rationally assigned, of achieving a given performance—, while attitude is attributable both to the cognitive and the emotional sphere—for example, prejudice as the ultimate determinant of choice behavior (Andersen & Kumar, 2006; Brown, Cobb, & Lusch, 2006).

15. An explicit link to the discrepancy theory and to Lewin's school of research would have probably allowed to adopt, right from the start, a "relational" perspective, including in the research on customer satisfaction the topic of trust in market relationships, hence highlighting the evolutionary process of the interaction between customer and company.
16. In this regard, see: Oliver (1980, 1981), Churchill and Suprenant (1982), Tse and Wilson (1988), Oliver (1997), and Fournier and Mick (1999).
17. In the literature on services marketing, the term "service encounter" is precisely used to describe the interaction between a customer and his service provider.
18. Relationship marketing has thoroughly studied the determinants of long-term collaborative relationships, although it is possible to identify multidisciplinary theoretical matrices in the approach to the topic. Both in the identification of the constructs and in the definition of the methods of operationalization and measurement, in fact, the study of market relations has been influenced by models on interpersonal relations and group dynamics (Thibaut & Kelley, 1959), studies on economic sociology (Granovetter, 1985), and those on social networks (Boissevain & Mitchell, 1973; Burt, 1992; Burt & Minor, 1982).
19. In the literature on relationship marketing, the dyadic exchange relationship has been considered the primary unit of analysis, whereas the object of the exchange evolves during the development of the relationship, and this in turn is influenced by the network of current and potential relationships of the actors in the dyad. Also as part of these studies, the management

literature has been devoted to the analysis of supply networks, especially among industrial enterprises.

20. Moreover, the centrality of trust in market relations is evidenced by several research studies aiming at defining their size and operationalizing their construct, and identifying antecedents and consequences (Blois, 1999).
21. The authors who considered trust as a multidimensional construct are numerous. Among others, Moorman et al. (1992) identified two dimensions, a cognitive dimension (conviction of reliability) and a behavioral dimension (intention/act of trust that leads one to become vulnerable), even if Morgan and Hunt (1994) later considered the second dimension as implicit in the first, suggesting to use it more effectively as an indicator of trust. Also Andaleeb (1992) suggested the use of two constructs, utilized however to identify different types of trust, closely connected to one another, and not explicitly operationalized as its dimensions: trust is defined as a function of ability and motivation perceived in the counterparty. With the same conceptual approach, Busacca and Castaldo (1996) suggested, instead, a three-dimensional definition of the construct, considering both the conviction of reliability and the perceptions regarding capabilities, and those related to nonopportunistic motives of the counterparty. In this regard, it should be noted that, from the perspective of the customer's buying behavior, the satisfaction construct, from which the dimension of trust originates, on which there is convergence of all the scholars (reliability), derives from the comparison between expectations of value and those of perceived value. The creation of the first is certainly influenced by the perceived ability of the company—in all probability compared with the offer alternatives already available in the process of creation of expectations prior to purchase—while the perception of value implies a new judgment (this time post-purchase) on that ability, but it also involves the evaluation of the fairness of the terms of trade, and therefore the motivation (opportunistic or not) of the company. In summary, it can be assumed that the dimension of trust reliability, resulting from satisfaction accumulated over time, encompasses in itself all the other dimensions proposed by the literature, to be considered, at times, as determinants (ability and motivation), at others as consequences (the intention or the action of trust) of trust itself.
22. With regard to commitment, defined as the "enduring desire of maintaining a serious relationship" and considered an antecedent of loyalty, Morgan and Hunt (1994) identified as determinants: trust, the degree of commonality of values between a company and a customer, the level of commonality of the purposes of the relationship—otherwise definable as goal congruence—, and the value of the benefits arising from the relationship, as well as the level of costs that its interruption could cause.
23. Cooperation, which should be considered an element of utmost importance, as well as trust, has been mainly studied in the context of partner relationships

and alliances between companies, showing again that cooperative attitudes are derived from high levels of satisfaction experienced in the course of transactions (Anderson & Narus, 1984, 1990). In general, moreover, it has been shown that a cooperative attitude is demonstrated also by the adoption of nonopportunistic behavior, not designed to maximize self-interest in the short term, on the basis of behavioral reciprocity expected in the future by the counterparty (Anderson & Weitz, 1989; Ganesan, 1994; Kumar, 1996; Mohr & Speckman, 1994). In this sense, several authors have shown that reciprocity and evolutionary forms of partnership largely depend on the perception of nonopportunism and on the more general commonality of values, or at least on perceptions of goal congruence (Lanza, 1998, 1999).

24. Models and evidence regarding the life cycle of the relationship were also proposed by Gronroos (1990), Deighton and Grayson (1995), Fontenot and Wilson (1997), and Iacobucci and Zerrillo (1997).
25. Among the different contributions examined, the authors emphasize the originality of the studies by Tuckman (1965), a social psychologist who studied the dynamics of interpersonal relationships: he focused on the conditions of transition from one phase of the cycle to the next, highlighting the decisive role of "conflicts in their initial state". Basically, in Tuckman's model, an evolutionary path of dyadic relationships emerges, which is defined by certain phases of verification, that would qualify as potential conflicts, the positive solution of which would result in strengthened relationships, followed by subsequent steps toward the evolutionary phases.
26. March (1994) identified, in particular, four cognitive constraints: (a) problems of attention, that is, the time and low capacity of attention of an individual; (b) memory problems, namely the limited ability to store and retrieve information in memory; (c) problems of understanding, meaning difficulty, by an individual, to organize information in order to connect it and interpret it correctly; (d) communication problems, linked to the possession of interpretive schemes diversified among different groups and cultures.
27. Nisbett and Ross (1980) identify two types of tools available to an individual, both to make decisions and to carry out the inferential processes: knowledge structures and judgment heuristics. The first represent all types of cognitive schemas, further discussed in the following section. The latter can be found in all the strategies that consider the completion of a successful action as the result of learning built on acquired experience. Through heuristics, individuals involved in the decision-making process recognize in the situations they face the recurring elements of situations that already occurred in the past, and after understanding them, they apply rules of proper behavior. These interpretative grids are part of the conscious and unconscious repertoires of individuals and develop through early experiences (Kahneman & Tversky, 1973; March, 1994).
28. With regard to the type of cost in question, see also Heskett et al. (1990).

29. With regard to the type of cost in question, see also Zeithaml et al. (1985).
30. Aaker (1991) defined this type of cost as the risk of change and stated that, even in the case a customer experiences problems with his current supplier, there is always the risk that the new one is worse. Such a meaning refers also to the concept of "inertia". In 1967, Bauer had proposed the notion of "lethargy towards the brand" in order to provide an explanation of customer loyalty toward the brand. The observation underlying this definition is that the effort it takes a customer to change brand is high and he does not receive any benefit from this action. Bauer (1967), as Tucker (1964) had previously done, postulated that lethargy, inertia, and habit are potential explanatory factors of loyalty. Few empirical studies provide support to the assertions of these authors, but among these, Exter (1986) shows that individuals develop loyalty to the products they buy because of inertia. Actually, Aaker (1991, p. 49) stated, "in many situations, it is difficult to get rid of customers, send them to competitors. The reason is that consumers do not like change, change requires effort, especially if the decision involves a high investment or risk." A similar concept underlies the observations by Shapiro and Varian (1999), with regard to the lock-in cycle in a digital environment. The perspective of this study, however, attempts to reverse this concept: resistance to change is not driven by inertia, but by satisfaction from a learned shopping script.
31. In the present study, learning costs are treated from a perspective which is more responsive to the digital economy; in particular, they are related to the use of the website by a business customer and learning the shopping script that maximizes its utility function.
32. In this regard, the authors write that "pre-switching search and evaluation costs represent consumer perceptions of the time and effort involved in seeking out information about available alternatives and evaluating their viability prior to switching" (Jones et al., 2002, p. 443). Research costs are costs that are associated with the research and evaluation of a new supplier. Empirical research designed to evaluate the relationship between research costs and customer buying behavior are still very limited. Among these, Lee and Cunningham (1994) are one of the few authors to have empirically demonstrated the existence of a positive relationship between the level of perceived switching costs and that of customer loyalty to a company.
33. The authors write, "Consumer perceptions of the time and effort needed to acquire and adapt to these new procedures and routines are referred to as post-switching behavioral and cognitive costs" (Jones et al., 2002, p. 443).
34. The description of these costs in the study by Jones et al. (2002, p. 443) is "[p]erception of the time, effort and expense of relaying needs and information to provider subsequent to switching".
35. Empirical research on the influence of learning costs on customer loyalty is still scarce. Gremler (1995) is one of the few authors to include the concept of switching costs among the antecedents of customer loyalty.

36. Classically, switching costs have been regarded with a negative connotation, as an advocate of an essentially behavioral trust, inertial but not cognitive (Shapiro & Varian, 1999). This concept was the basis for the development of lock-in strategies. This study, however, seeks to overturn this perspective, starting from the satisfaction in the shopping experience, which can be found in the acquisition of a script that would be too costly to lose.
37. In this sense, a script is a structure that basically contains two types of knowledge: a sequence of actions and a set of roles. After recognizing a situation and retrieving the corresponding script, the sequence of actions (or "scenes") allows to perform "anticipatory" elaboration ("expecting certain things to happen"). Thanks to this elaboration, expecting the occurrence of certain events, it will be easier for an individual to recognize those events.
38. Several studies (Abbot et al., 1985; Bower et al., 1979; Lichtenstein & Brewer, 1980) have allowed to better understand the features of scripts, highlighting very clearly the differences with respect to other types of schemas.
39. From a computational point of view, scripts are an important simplification to account for the very short time required by the mind to determine which action has to be performed after another action. From a psychological point of view, however, scripts are not consistent with the observations of Gordon Bower, who already had in 1971 pointed out the empirical evidence of some sort of serial processing but had also noticed and studied the phenomenon of "confusion". According to Bower, scenes of a script can be used by multiple scripts: for example, the scene of queueing up in a bank and the scene of queueing up at the post office are the same scene, which belongs as much to the script of going to the bank as to the script of going to the post office. This can give rise to the phenomenon of confusion: a subject can confuse one script with another that admits the same scene. To overcome the psychological implausibility of the scripts reported by Bower, Schank introduced in the eighties the memory organization packets, or MOP, which essentially have the same purpose, but do not contain all the knowledge they use; they contain only a reference to such knowledge (Schank, 1984).
40. In general terms, marketing and organizational behavior were the fields of study that most widely used concepts borrowed from research in cognitive psychology. In particular, with regard to research on organizational behavior, although the contributions in the field are still few in number, one of the first works on the subject was the contribution by Gioia and Poole (1984), who investigated the repetition of certain activities of an organization and the development of stereotyped actions that make it easy to apply the concept of script to the study of the organization's cognitive and behavioral relationships. The authors refer, in particular, to the suitability of the script to describe and understand different aspects of organizational behavior

(such as selection procedures, the decision-making processes for the choice of a new employee, the process of learning, etc.) The concept of learning within the organization was thoroughly analyzed in a later work by Gioia and Manz (1985): a person hired by a company must learn a behavioral script that is transferred by those already working for that company (as it occurs with the instruction and training of employees). One of the studies that has most inspired this research is certainly Woofford's work (1994): knowledge of organizational procedures, the cognitive processes underlying the actions, and the decision-making processes are memorized by individuals in the form of scripts. Among these, known scripts are used to approach relatively simple problems; new scripts, instead, are used in the case of situations in which the gap between the performance and the objective is larger. Finally, also Tansik and Smith's work (1991) is of great interest: the repetition of actions allows the script to become a customary behavior. Once the script is done automatically, the individual's cognitive effort will be reduced. Also significant are the latest studies on the attitude of scripts to transfer the cognitive map of a company through the creation of spin-offs (Del Giudice, Della Peruta, Maggioni, 2013a, Campanella, Della Peruta, Del Giudice, 2013a; Campanella, Della Peruta, Del Giudice, 2013b; Del Giudice, Della Peruta, Maggioni, 2013b; Del Giudice, Della Peruta, Carayannis 2013; Del Giudice, Della Peruta, Maggioni, 2013c).

41. The author, studying the various attitudes that a customer may assume when purchasing a good, identified three different types: consumer recognition, consumer preference, and consumer insistence. The first case occurs when the customer, other things being equal, tends to choose a recognized brand (both for previous positive consumption experiences and as a result of advertising that struck him favorably) among other brands and unbranded products. In the second case, the customer shows the intention of choosing a particular brand regardless of the store's stock assortment: this situation is typical of convenience goods, and in the event the customer cannot find the brand he wants, he is well prepared to choose another one with similar characteristics. In the last case, instead, the customer shows a strong intention of buying a particular brand and is not willing to accept substitute products. This is the case of purchases of so-called speciality goods, which are strongly characterized in terms of quality, special features, and specific services.
42. The first authors who pointed out the need to distinguish different forms of loyalty—albeit in different contexts of study and with different purposes—were Hirschman (1970) and Day (1970). The latter, in particular, was the first to theorize the evidence of forms of so-called "spurious" loyalty, which is only apparently such because these forms are not determined by a clear, direct, and controllable relationship between the subject and the object of loyalty (the brand or the company).

43. The cognitive dimension involves the attitudinal aspect of the buying process, that is, the attitude that a customer shows about the possibility of using only one supplier compared with the opposite hypothesis of dealing with many (switching behavior). In essence, the dimension refers to the trust placed by a customer in a company; loyalty reaches high levels when the customer's will is directed to a single supplier, despite the attractive actions taken by competitors.
44. This condition, according to the authors, identifies buyers' "*happenstance*", an uncommon term that is intended to emphasize the buyer's position "without intention", a sort of lack of shopping planning, which would not occur, therefore, as a consequence of preference attitudes consistent with choice behavior (Fishbein & Ajzen, 1975).
45. From the same perspective, all studies carried out to define measurements of the construct of "behavioral loyalty" should be mentioned (Busacca & Castaldo, 1996).
46. The cognitive dimension of loyalty is associated with satisfaction (Day, 1970), attitudes (Dick & Basu, 1994; Jacoby & Chestnut, 1978), and trust (Busacca & Castaldo, 1996).
47. In particular, according to the two authors, only when the company's offer manages to reach the maximum behavioral and cognitive values of loyalty is it possible to talk about absolute loyalty.
48. The forms of latent loyalty may be explained by the known phenomena of high loyalty to a group of brands and by the consequent difficulty of determining unequivocally the penetration levels that define a brand as focal. In some cases characterized by buying behavior seeking assortment, the different brands, which are more than substitutes, can be considered complementary compared with the need of assortment. Other interpretations of this form of loyalty are related to situational factors that influence behavior, even beyond very positive attitudes toward the brand (locational disadvantages, constraints of time or income, other family priorities, etc.).
49. Also in these cases, the explanation of this form of loyalty lies in situational factors such as temporary convenience or in buying behavior seeking assortment.
50. These interpretations of loyalty, however, do not examine the dynamic perspective of the process that binds a customer to a company during the entire life cycle of the relationship.
51. Also Payne (1997), when analyzing in-depth the topic of the relationships between customers and businesses, identified different customer profiles and varying levels of loyalty; in particular, through the construction of so-called "customer ladder", he identified different relationship intensities on different "steps" of the relationship (from a potential buyer to its partner, via the customer, the supporter, the lawyer, etc.).

Bibliography

Adrian Payne (1997) Services Marketing, Prentice Hall Leon G. Schiffman.

Bion, W. R. (2013). Experiences in groups: And other papers. New York: Routledge.

Gersick, C. J. (1988). Time and transition in work teams: Toward a new model of group development. *Academy of Management journal, 31*(1), 9–41.

Yalom, I. D., & Leszcz, M. (2005). The theory and practice of group psychotherapy. New York: Basic Books.

Darroch, J. (2005). Knowledge management, innovation and firm performance. *Journal of knowledge management, 9*(3), 101–115.

Palacios Marqués, D., & José Garrigós Simón, F. (2006). The effect of knowledge management practices on firm performance. *Journal of Knowledge Management, 10*(3), 143–156.

Smith, A. D., & Rupp, W. T. (2002). Communication and loyalty among knowledge workers: a resource of the firm theory view. *Journal of knowledge management, 6*(3), 250–261.

Rowley, J. (2002). Eight questions for customer knowledge management in e-business. *Journal of knowledge management, 6*(5), 500–511. Chaudhuri, A., & Holbrook, M. B. (2001). The chain of effects from brand trust and brand affect to brand performance: the role of brand loyalty. *Journal of marketing, 65*(2), 81–93.

Chaudhuri, A., & Holbrook, M. B. (2001). The chain of effects from brand trust and brand affect to brand performance: the role of brand loyalty. *Journal of marketing, 65*(2), 81–93.

Hollensen, S. (2015) Marketing Management: A Relationship Approach. Harlow: Pearson Education.

Palmatier, R. W., Jarvis, C. B., Bechkoff, J. R., & Kardes, F. R. (2009). The role of customer gratitude in relationship marketing. *Journal of marketing, 73*(5), 1–18.

Aaker, D. (1991). *Managing brand equity. Capitalizing on the value of a brand name*. New York: The Free Press.

Kotler, P., Burton, S., Deans, K., Brown, L., & Armstrong, G. (2015). Marketing. Pearson Higher Education.

Saeidi, S. P., Sofian, S., Saeidi, P., Saeidi, S. P., & Saaeidi, S. A. (2015). How does corporate social responsibility contribute to firm financial performance? The mediating role of competitive advantage, reputation, and customer satisfaction. *Journal of Business Research, 68*(2), 341–350.

Davcik, N. S., & Sharma, P. (2015). Impact of product differentiation, marketing investments and brand equity on pricing strategies: A brand level investigation. *European Journal of Marketing, 49*(5/6), 760–781.

Abbott, V., Black, J., & Smith, E. (1985). The representation of scripts in memory. *Journal of Memory and Language, 24*, 179–199.

Del Giudice M., Della Peruta M.R., Maggioni V. (2013), Collective knowledge and organizational routines within academic communities of practice: an empirical research on science-entrepreneurs, *Journal of the Knowledge Economy, 4*(3), 260–278.

Campanella F., Della Peruta M.R., Del Giudice M. (2013). The role of socio-cultural background on the characteristics and the financing of youth entrepreneurship. An exploratory study of university graduates in Italy, *Journal of the Knowledge Economy, 4*(3), 244–259.

Campanella F., Della Peruta M.R., Del Giudice M. (2013), Informational approach of family spin-offs in the funding process of innovative projects: an empirical verification, *Journal Of Innovation And Entrepreneurship, 2*(18), DOI: 10.1186/2192-5372-2-18.

Del Giudice M., Della Peruta M.R., Maggioni V. (2013). The "right" knowledge and spin-off processes: an empirical analysis on knowledge transfer, *Journal of the Knowledge Economy, 4*(3), 304–318.

Del Giudice M., Della Peruta M.R., Carayannis E. (2013), Unpacking Open Innovation. Highlights from a Co-Evolutionary Inquiry, Palgrave Macmillan, New York.

Del Giudice M., Della Peruta M.R., Maggioni V. (2013), Spontaneous processes of reproduction of family-based entrepreneurship: an empirical research on the cognitive nature of the spin-offs, *Journal of Innovation and Entrepreneurship, 2*(12), DOI: 10.1186/2192-5372-2-12.

Abelson, R. (1976). Script processing in attitude formation and decision making. In J. S. Carrol & J. W. Payne (Eds.), *Cognition and social behavior* (pp. 33–45). Hillsdale, NJ: Erlbaum.

Abelson, R. (1981). Psychological status of the script concept. *American Psychologist, 36*(7), 715–729.

Alford, B. (1998). Using cognitive scripts to assess the process of professional service delivery. *Journal of Professional Services Marketing, 17*(1), 77–103.

Andaleeb, S. S. (1992). The trust concept: Research issues for channel distribution. In J. N.Shteh (Ed.), *Research in marketing* (Vol. 11, pp. 1–34). Greenwich, CT: Jai Press.

Anderson, R. E. (1973). Consumer dissatisfaction: The effect of disconfirmed expectancy on perceived product performance. *Journal of marketing research*, 38–44.

Andersen, P. H., & Kumar, R. (2006). Emotions, trust and relationship development in business relationships: A conceptual model for buyer-seller dyads. *Industrial Marketing Management, 35*(4), 522–535.

East, R., Wright, M. & Vanhuele, M. (2013) "Consumer Behaviour: Applications in Marketing" 2nd edition, SAGE.

Lantos, G. P. (2015). Consumer behavior in action: Real-life applications for marketing managers. Routledge.

Anderson, J. C., & Narus, J. A. (1984). A model of distributor's perspective of distributor-manufacturer working relationships. *Journal of Marketing, 48*(Fall), 62–74.
Anderson, J. C., & Narus, J. A. (1990). A model of distributor firm and manufacturer firm working partnership. *Journal of Marketing, 54*(January), 44–53.
Anderson, J. C., & Weitz, B. (1989). Determinants of continuity in conventional industrial channel dyads. *Marketing Science, 8*(Fall), 310–323.
Assael, H. (1995). *Consumer behavior and marketing action.* Cincinnati: South Western College Publishing.
Bagozzi, R. P. (1974). Marketing as an organized behavioral system of exchange. *Journal of Marketing, 38*(October), 77–81.
Bagozzi, R. P. (1975). Marketing as exchange. *Journal of Marketing, 39*(October), 32–39.
Ball, D., Coelho, P. S., & Machás, A. (2004). The role of communication and trust in explaining customer loyalty: An extension to the ECSI model. *European Journal of Marketing, 38*(9/10), 1272–1293.
Bandura, A. (1982). Self-efficacy: Mechanism in human agency. *American Psychologist, 37*, 122–147.
Bandura, A. (1986). The explanatory and predictive scope of self-efficacy theory. *Journal of Social and Clinical Psychology, 4*, 359–373.
Bang, V. V., & Joshi, S. L. (2010). Market expansion strategy–performance relationship. *Journal of Strategic Marketing, 18*(1), 57–75.
Barlett, F. (1932). *Remembering.* Cambridge, UK: Cambridge University Press.
Barney, J., & Ouchi, W. (1984). Information cost and organizational governance. *Management Science,* 10. (Trad. It., Costi delle informazioni e strutture economiche di governo delle transizioni. In R. Nacamulli & A. Rugiadini (a cura di), *Organizzazione e Mercato*, Il Mulino, Bologna, 1985).
Bateson, J. (1985, Fall). Self-service consumer. An exploratory study. *Journal of Retailing*, 61(3), 49–76.
Bauer, R. (1967). Consumer behavior as risk taking. In D. F. Cox (Ed.), *Risk taking and information handling in consumer behavior* (pp. 23–33). Boston: Division of Research, Harvard University.
Berry, L. (1983). Relationship marketing. In L. Berry, L. Shostack, & G. Upah (Eds.), *Emerging perspectives on services marketing* (pp. 25–28). Chicago: AMA.
Berry, L. L., & Parasuraman, A. (1991). *Marketing services.* New York: The Free Press.
Bitner, M. J. (1995). Building service relationship: It's all about promises. *Journal of the Academy of Marketing Science, 23*(Fall), 236–245.
Blois, K. J. (1999). Trust in business to business relationships. An evalutation of its status. *Journal of Management Studies, 36*(2), 197–215.
Boissevain, J., & Mitchell, J. C. (Eds.) (1973). *Network analysis: Studies in human interaction.* The Hague-Paris: Mouton.

Bower, G., Black, J., & Turner, T. (1979). Script memory for text. *Cognitive Psychology, 11*, 177–220.

Bozinoff, L., & Roth, V. (1983). Recognition memory for script activities: An energy conservation application. In R. Bagozzi & A. Tybout (Eds.), *Advances in Consumer Research, vol. 10, Proceedings of the 13th Annual Conference* (pp. 655–660). Ann Aror, MI: Association for Consumer Research.

Brown, J. R., Cobb, A. T., & Lusch, R. F. (2006). The role played by interorganizational contracts and justice in marketing channel relationship. *Journal of Business Research, 59*(2), 166–175.

Brüggen, E. C., Foubert, B., & Gremler, D. D. (2011). Extreme makeover: Short- and long-term effects of a remodeled servicescape. *Journal of Marketing, 75*(5), 71–87.

Bucklin, L. P., & Sengupta, S. (1993). Organizing successful co-marketing alliances. *Journal of Marketing, 57*(April), 32–46.

Burt, R. S. (1992). *Structural holes: The social structure of competition*. Cambridge, MA: Harvard University Press.

Burt, R. S., & Minor, M. J. (Eds.) (1982). *Applied network analysis: Structural methodology for empirical social research*. Beverly Hills, CA: Sage.

Busacca, B., & Castaldo, S. (1996). *Il potenziale competitivo della fedeltà alla marca e all'insegna commerciale. Una metodologia di misurazione congiunta*. Milano: Egea.

Cardozo, R. N. (1965). An experimental study of consumer effort, expectation and satisfaction. *Journal of Marketing Research, 2*(August), 244–249.

Chen, P. T., & Hu, H. H. (2010). The effect of relational benefits on perceived value in relation to customer loyalty: An empirical study in the Australian coffee outlets industry. *International journal of hospitality management, 29*(3), 405–412.

Dacko, S. (2008). The advanced dictionary of marketing: putting theory to use. Oxford University Press.

Terrill, C., & Middlebrooks, A. (2000). Market leadership strategies for service companies: Creating growth, profits, and customer loyalty. McGraw Hill Professional.

Tzokas, N., & Saren, M. (2004). Competitive advantage, knowledge and relationship marketing: where, what and how?. *Journal of Business & Industrial Marketing, 19*(2), 124–135.

Babin, B. J., & Zikmund, W. G. (2015). Essentials of marketing research. Nelson Education.

Chaarlas, L. J., Rajkumar, R., Kogila, N., Lydia, J., & Noorunisha, A. (2012). Service related issues faced by clients - The major cause behind brand switching in cellular phone service industry. *Arabian Journal of Business and Management Review (Oman Chapter), 1*(8), 33–46.

Chandrashekaran, M., Rotte, K., Tax, S. S., & Grewal, R. (2007). Satisfaction strength and customer loyalty. *Journal of Marketing Research, 44*(1), 153–163.

Churchill, G. A., & Suprenant, C. (1982). An investigation into the determinants of customer satisfaction. *Journal of Marketing Research, 19*(November), 491–504.

Coase, R. (1937). The nature of the firm. *Economica, 4*, 386–405.

Copeland, M. T. (1923). Relation of consumer's buying habits to marketing methods. *Harward Business Review, 1*(April), 282–289.

Costabile M., 1998, Customer Satisfaction and Trust into the Resource-based Perspective. Research Propositions Endorsing the Confirmation/ Disconfirmation Paradigm, Andersson P. (edit by),"Market Relationships", Track 1, Proceedings of the European Marketing Academy, pp. 76–97.

Crosby, L. A., Evans, K. R., & Cowles, D. (1990). Relationship quality in services selling: An interpersonal influence perspective. *Journal of Marketing, 54*(July), 68–81.

Day, G. S. (1970). *Buyer attitudes and brand choice behavior*. New York: The Free Press.

Day, G. S., & Wensley, R. (1983). Marketing theory with a strategic orientation. *Journal of Marketing, 47*(4), 78–89.

Deighton, J., & Grayson, K. (1995). Marketing and seduction: Building exchange relationship by managing social consensus. *Journal of Consumer Research, 21*(March), 660–676.

Del Giudice, M. (2004). Turning web surfers into loyal customers: Cognitive lock-in through interface design and website usability. In Y. Gao (Ed.), *Web systems design and online consumer behavior*. New York and Hershey, PA: Idea Publishers.

Del Giudice M., Della Peruta M.R., Maggioni V. (2013a), Collective knowledge and organizational routines within academic communities of practice: an empirical research on science-entrepreneurs, *Journal of the Knowledge Economy, 4*(3), 260–278.

Campanella F., Della Peruta M.R., Del Giudice M. (2013a). The role of sociocultural background on the characteristics and the financing of youth entrepreneurship. An exploratory study of university graduates in Italy, *Journal of the Knowledge Economy, 4*(3), 244–259.

Campanella F., Della Peruta M.R., Del Giudice M. (2013b), Informational approach of family spin-offs in the funding process of innovative projects: an empirical verification, *Journal Of Innovation And Entrepreneurship, 2*(18), DOI: 10.1186/2192-5372-2-18.

Del Giudice M., Della Peruta M.R., Maggioni V. (2013b). The "right" knowledge and spin-off processes: an empirical analysis on knowledge transfer, *Journal of the Knowledge Economy, 4*(3), 304–318.

Del Giudice M., Della Peruta M.R., Carayannis E. (2013), Unpacking Open Innovation. Highlights from a Co-Evolutionary Inquiry, Palgrave Macmillan, New York, ISBN: 978-1-137-35932-2.

Del Giudice M., Della Peruta M.R., Maggioni V. (2013c), Spontaneous processes of reproduction of family-based entrepreneurship: an empirical research on the cognitive nature of the spin-offs, *Journal of Innovation and Entrepreneurship, 2*(12), DOI: 10.1186/2192-5372-2-12

Dick, A. S., & Basu, K. (1994). Customer loyalty: Toward an integrated conceptual framework. *Journal of the Academy of Marketing Science, 22*(Winter), 99–113.

Dwyer, F. R., Schurr, P. H., & Oh, S. (1987). Developing buyer and seller relationships. *Journal of Marketing, 51*(April), 11–27.

Engel, J. F., Kollat, D. T., & Blackwell, R. D. (1968). *Consumer behavior.* New York: Holt Rinehart & Winston.

Exter, T. (1986). Looking for brand loyalty. *American Demographics, 8*(April), 32–33, pp. 52–56.

Farber-Canziani, B. (1997). Leveraging customer competency in service firms. *International Journal of Service Industry Management, 8*(1), 5–25.

Farrell, J., & Shapiro, C. (1988). Dynamic competition with switching costs. *RAND Journal of Economics, 19*(1), 123–137.

Fishbein, M., & Ajzen, I. (1975). *Belief, attitude, intention and behavior: An introduction to theory and research.* Reading, MA: Addison-Wesley.

Fisk, S., & Taylor, S. (1991). *Social cognition.* New York: McGraw-Hill.

Fletcher, K. P., & Peters, L. D. (1997). Trust and direct marketing enviroments: A consumer perspective. *Journal of Marketing Management, 13*, 523–539.

Fontenot, R. J., & Wilson, E. J. (1997). Relational exchange: A review of selected models for a prediction matrix of relationship activities. *Journal of Business Research, 39*, 5–12.

Foray, D., & Steinmueller, W. E. (2003). The economics of knowledge reproduction by inscription. *Industrial and Corporate Change, 2*, 299–319.

Ford, D. (1980). The development of buyer-seller relationships. *European Journal of Marketing, 14*(5), 339–353.

Ford, D. (Ed.) (1998). *Managing business relationships.* Chichester: Wiley.

Fornell, C. (1992). A national customer satisfaction barometer: The Swedish experience. *Journal of Marketing, 56*(January), 6–21.

Fournier, S., & Mick, D. G. (1999). Rediscovering satisfaction. *Journal of Marketing, 63*(October), 5–23.

Ganesan, S. (1994). Determinants of long-term orientation in buyer-seller relationship. *Journal of Marketing, 58*(April), 1–19.

Gijsbrechts, E., Heerde, H. J. v., & Pauwels, K. (2008). Winners and losers in a major price war. *Journal of Marketing Research, 45*(October), 499–518.

Gioia, D. A., & Manz, C. (1985). Linking cognition and behavior. A script processing interpretation of vicarious learning. *Academy of Management Review, 10*(3), 527–539.

Gioia, D. A., & Poole, P. P. (1984). Scripts in organizational behaviour. *Academy of Management Review, 10*(3), 527–539.

Granovetter, M. (1985). Economic action and social structure: The problem of embeddedness. *American Journal of Sociology, 91*, 481–510.
Grayson, K., & Ambler, T. (1999). The dark side of long-term relationships in marketing services. *Journal of Marketing Research, 36*, 132–141.
Gremler, D. (1995). *The effect of satisfaction, switching costs and interpersonal bonds on service loyalty*. Unpublished doctoral dissertation, Arizona State University.
Grönroos, C. (1983). Innovative marketing strategies and organizations structures for service firms. In L. Berry, L. Shostack, & G. Upah (Eds.), *Emerging perspectives on services marketing* (pp. 9–21). Chicago: AMA.
Grönroos, C. (1990). *Service management and marketing: Managing the moment of truth in service competition*. Lexington, MA: Lexington.
Grönroos, C. (1994a). Quo Vadis marketing? Toward a relationship marketing approach. *Journal of Marketing Management, 10*, 347–360.
Grönroos, C. (1994b). From marketing mix to relationship marketing: Towards a paradigm shift in marketing. *Management Decision, 32*, 4–20.
Gruen, T. W. (1995). The outcome set of relationship marketing in consumer marketing. *International Business Review, 4*, 447–469.
Guiltinan, J. (1989). A classification of switching costs with implications for relationship marketing. In T. Childers, R. Bagozzi, J. Peter, et al. (Eds.), *AMA winter educators' conference: Marketing theory and practice* (pp. 216–220). Chicago: AMA.
Gummesson, E. (1987). The new marketing—Developing long-term interactive relationships. *Long Range Planning, 20*(4), 10–20.
Gurviez, P. (1996). The trust concept in the brand-consumer relationship. In J. Beràcs, A. Bauer, & J. Simon (Eds.), "Marketing for an expanding europe", Proceedings of the 25th EMAC Conference European Marketing Academy, Budapest (Vol. I, pp. 559–574).
Hakansson, H., & Wootz, B. (1979). A framework of industrial buying and selling. *Industrial Marketing Management, 8*(1), 28–39.
Heskett, J., Sasser, W., & Hart, C. (1990). *Service breakthroughs: Changing the rules of the game*. New York: The Free Press.
Hirschman, A. O. (1970). *Exit, voice and loyalty. Responses to declines in firms, organizations and states*. Cambridge, MA: Harvard University Press.
Hoppe, E. (1930). Ergfolg und Misserfolg. *Psicologische Forschung, XIV*, 1–62.
Howard, J. (1963). *Marketing management: Analysis and planning*. Homewood: Irwin.
Howard, J., & Sheth, J. N. (1969). *The theory of buyer behavior*. New York, NY: Wiley.
Hsu, T., & Chiang, C. (2011). Script comparisons during service encounters in fast-food chains. *Tourism and Hospitality Research, 11*(January), 19–29.
Hubbert, A., Garcia Sehorn, A., & Brown, S. (1995). Service expectations: The consumer versus the provider. *International Journal of Consumer Research, 6*(1), 6–21.

Hunt, K. H. (Ed.). (1977). *Conceptualization and measurement of consumer satisfaction/dissatisfaction*. Report No. 77–103. Cambridge, MA: Marketing Science Institute.

Hutt, M. D., & Speh, T. W. (2012). *Business marketing management: B2B*. Cengage Learning.

Iacobucci, D., Grayson, K., & Omstrom, A. (1992). The calculus of service quality and customer satisfaction. *Working Paper*. J. L. Kellogg Graduate School of Management, Northwestern University, Evanston.

Iacobucci, D., & Zerrillo, P. (1997). *The relationship life cycle: A network-dyad-network dynamic conceptualization and the application of some classic psychological theories to its management* (Vol. 13, pp. 47–68). Jai Press.

Iasevoli, G. (2000). *Il valore del cliente. Misurare gli effetti della soddisfazione e della fedeltà sul valore dell'impresa*. Milano: FrancoAngeli.

Iederan, O. C., Curseu, P. L., Vermeulen, P. A. M., & Geurts, J. L. A. (2011). Cognitive representations of institutional change: Similarities and dissimilarities in the cognitive schema of entrepreneurs. *Journal of Organizational Change Management, 24*(1), 9–28.

Jackson, B. (1985). Build customer relationships that last. *Harvard Business Review, 63*(November–December), 120–128.

Jacobs, B., & De Klerk, H. M. (2010). Online apparel shopping behaviour of South African professional women: The role of consumers' apparel shopping scripts. *International Journal of Consumer Studies, 34*, 255–264.

Jacoby, J. (1971). Brand loyalty: A conceptual definition. *American Psychological Association Proceedings, 6*, 655–656.

Jacoby, J., & Chestnut, R. W. (1978). *Brand loyalty. Measurement and management*. New York, NY: Wiley.

Jacoby, J., & Kyner, D. B. (1973). Brand loyalty vs. repeat purchaising behavior. *Journal of Marketing Research, 10*(February), 1–9.

Jones, M. A., Mothersbaugh, D. L., & Beatty, S. E. (2002). Why customers stay: Measuring the underlying dimensions of services switching costs and managing their differential strategic outcomes. *Journal of Business Research, 55*, 441–450.

Kahneman, D., & Tversky, A. (1973). On the psychology of prediction. *Psychological Review, 80*, 237–251.

Klemperer, P. (1987a). Markets with consumer switching costs. *Quarterly Journal of Economics, 102*, 375–394.

Klemperer, P. (1987b). The competitiveness of markets with switching costs. *RAND Journal of Economics, 18*(1), 138–150.

Kotler, P., & Levy, S. J. (1969). Broadening the concept of marketing. *Journal of Marketing, 33*(July), 10–15.

Krumske, W. (1987). Marketing strategies for pricing services: An application in the deregulated financial service industry. Unpublished doctoral dissertation, University of Illinois at Urbana-Champaign.

Rigby, D., & Bilodeau, B. (2015). Management tools & trends 2015. London, Bain & Company.
Kumar, N. (1996). The power of trust in manufacturer-retailer relationship. *Harvard Business Review, 74*(November–December), 92–106.
Le Meunier-FitzHugh, K., & Lane, N. (2009). Collaboration between sales and marketing, market orientation and business performance in business-to-business organizations. *Journal of Strategic Marketing, 17*(3), 291–306.
Lechner, C., & Kreutzer, M. (2010). Coordinating growth initiatives in multi-unit firms. *Long Range Planning, 43*(1), 6–32.
Lee, C., & Cunningham, L. (1994). Assessing service quality as an effective management tool: The case of airline industry. *Journal of Marketing Theory and Practice, 2*(2), 79–96.
Lee, C., Huang, S., Barnes, F., & Kao, L. (2010). Business performance and customer relationship management: The effect of IT, organizational contingency and business process on Taiwanese manufacturers. *Total Quality Management & Business Excellence, 21*(1), 43–65.
Lee, H. H., & Kim, J. (2008). The effects of shopping orientations on consumers' satisfaction with product search and purchases in a multi-channel environment. *Journal of Fashion Marketing and Management, 12*(2), 193–216.
Leigh, T., & McGraw, P. (1989). Mapping the procedural knowledge of industrial sell personnel: A script-theoretic investigation. *Journal of Marketing, 53*(January), 16–34.
Kotler, P., Keller, K. L., Manceau, D., & Hémonnet-Goujot, A. (2015). Marketing management (Vol. 14). Englewood Cliffs, NJ: Prentice Hall.
Babin, B. J., & Zikmund, W. G. (2015). Essentials of marketing research. Nelson Education.
Leigh, T., & Rethans, A. (1983). Experiences with script elicitations within consumer decision making contexts. In R. Bagozzi & A. Tybout (Eds.), *Advances in consumer research* (vol. 10, pp. 667–672). Proceedings of the 13th Annual Conference, Association of Consumer research, Ann Arbor, MI.
Lewin, K. (1936). *Principles of topological psychology.* New York: McGraw Hill. (Trad. It., *Princìpi di Psicologia Topologica*, Firenze: Edizioni Organizzazioni Speciali, 1960).
Lichtenstein, E., & Brewer, W. (1980). Memory for goal-directed events. *Cognitive Psychology, 12*, 412–445.
Luhmann, N. (1989). Vertrauen. Ein Mechanismus der Reduktion sozialer Komplexität. 3rd edition, Stuttgart: Enke.
March, J. (1994). *A primer on decision making. How decision happen.* New York: The Free Press. (Trad. It., *Prendere decisioni*, Bologna: Il Mulino, 1998).
Marion, F. (1996). La partecipation du client à la réalisation du service en milieu inter-organisationnel, thèse pour le doctorat nouveau régime, ès-Sciences de Gestion, Université Jean Moulin Lyon III, Institut d'Administration des Entreprises.

Lovelock, C., & Patterson, P. (2015). Services marketing. Pearson Australia.

Masanell, R. C., & Ricart, J. E. (2010). From strategy to business models and onto tactics. *Long Range Planning, 43*(2), 195–215.

McGrath, R. G. (2010). Business models: A discovery driven approach. *Long Range Planning, 43*(2), 247–261.

Meng, J., & Elliott, K. M. (2009). Investigating structural relationships between service quality, switching costs, and customer satisfaction. *The Journal of Applied Business and Economics, 9*(2), 54–67.

Meng Leong, S., Busch, P., & Roedder, J. D. (1989). Knowledge base and salesperson effectiveness: A script theoretic analysis. *Journal of Marketing Research, 26*(May), 164–178.

Moe, W. W., & Yang, S. (2009). Inertial disruption: The impact of a new competitive entrant on online consumer search. *Journal of Marketing, 73*(January), 109–121.

Mohr, J., & Speckman, R. (1994). Characteristics of partnership success: Partnership attributes, communications behavior, and conflict resolution techniques. *Strategic Management Journal, 15*, 135–152.

Moorman, C., Deshpandè, R., & Zaltman, G. (1993). Factors affecting trust in market research relationship. *Journal of Marketing, 57*(January), 81–101.

Moorman, C., Zaltman, G., & Deshpandè, R. (1992). Relationships between providers and users of market research: The dynamics of trust within and between organizations. *Journal of Marketing Research, 29*(August), 314–328.

Morgan, R. M., & Hunt, S. D. (1994). The commitment-trust theory of relationship marketing. *Journal of Marketing, 58*(July), 20–38.

Murray, K. (1991). A test of services marketing theory: Consumer information acquisition activities. *Journal of Marketing, 55*(1), 10–25.

Newman, J. W., & Werbel, R. A. (1973). Multivariate analysis of brand loyalty for major household aplliances. *Journal of Marketing Research, 10*(November), 404–409.

Nicosia, F. (1966). *Consumer decision processes*. Englewood Cliffs: Prentice Hall.

Nisbett, R., & Ross, L. (1980). *Human inference: Strategies and shortcomings of social judgment.*

Nottenburg, G., & Shoben, E. (1980). Scripts as lineal orders. *Journal of Experimental Social Psychology, 16*, 329–347.

O'Sullivan, T. (2010). Dangling conversations: Web-forum use by a symphony orchestra's audience members. *Journal of Marketing Management, 26*(7), 656–670.

Oliver, R. L. (1977). Effect of expectation and disconfirmation on post-exposure product avaluations: An alternative interpretation. *Journal of Applied Psychology, 62*(4), 480–486.

Oliver, R. L. (1980). A cognitive model of the antecedents and consequences of satisfaction decisions. *Journal of Marketing Research, 17*(4), 460–469.

Oliver, R. L. (1981). Measurement and evaluation of satisfaction processes in retail setting. *Journal of Retailing, 57*(Fall), 25–48.
Oliver, R. L. (1997). *Satisfaction. A behavioral perspective on the consumer.* New York: McGraw Hill.
Oliver, R. L. (1999). Whence consumer loyalty. *Journal of Marketing, 63*(Special Issue), 33–44.
Olson, J. C., & Dover, P. A. (1979). Disconfirmation of consumer expectations through product trial. *Journal of Applied Psychology, 64*(2), 179–189.
Palmatier, R. W., Scheer, L. K., & Steenkamp, J. B. E. M. (2007). Customer loyalty to whom? Managing the benefits and risks of salesperson-owned loyalty. *Journal of Marketing Research, 44*(2), 185–199.
Parasuraman, A., Zeithaml, V. A., & Berry, L. L. (1989). SERVQUAL: A multiple item scale for measuring consumer perceptions of service quality. *Journal of Retailing,* (Spring), 12–39.
Peter, J. C., & Olson, J. C. (1996). *Consumer behavior and marketing strategy.* Homewood: Irwin.
Pil, F. K., & Holweg, M. (2006). Evolving from value chain to value grid. *Sloan Management Review, 47*(4), 72–80.
Porter, M. E. (1986). *Competitive advantage: Creating and sustaining superior performance.* New York: Free Press.
Reichheld, F. F. (1996). *The loyalty effect.* Boston: Harvard Business School Press.
Schank, R. (1984). *The cognitive computer: On language, learning and artificial intelligence.* Reading, MA: Addison-Wesley.
Schank, R., & Abelson, R. (1977). *Scripts, plans, goals and understanding.* Hillsdale, NJ: Erlbaum.
Schindehutte, M., Morris, M. H., & Kocak, A. (2008). Understanding market-driving behavior: The role of entrepreneurship. *Journal of Small Business Management, 46*(1), 4–26.
Selden, L., & MacMillan, I. C. (2006). Manage customer-centric innovation systematically. *Harvard Business Review, 84*(4), 108–116.
Shankar, V., Smith, A. K., & Rangaswamy, A. (2003). Customer satisfaction and loyalty in online and offline environments. *International Journal of Research in Marketing, 20*(2), 153–175.
Shapiro, C., & Varian, H. R. (1999). *Informatiom rules. A strategic guide to the network economy.* Boston: Harvard Business School Press.
Shurr, P. (1986). Four script studies: What we have learned. In R. Lutz (Ed.), *Advances for consumer research* (Vol. 13, pp. 498–503). Provo, UT: Association for Consumer Research.
Shurr, P. H., & Ozanne, J. L. (1985). Influence on exchange processes: Buyer's preconceptions of a seller's trustworthiness and bargaining toughness. *Journal of Consumer Research, 11*(March), 938–947.

Simon, H. (1977). *Models of discovery and other topics in the method of science.* Dordrecht: Reidell.

Sirmon, D. G., Hitt, M. A., Arregle, J. L., & Campbell, J. T. (2010). The dynamic interplay of capability strengths and weaknesses: Investigating the bases of temporary competitive advantage. *Strategic Management Journal, 31*, 1386–1409.

Soellner, A. (1994). Commitment in exchange relationships: The role of switching costs in building and sustaining competitive advantages. In J. Sheth & A. Parvatiyar (Eds.), *Relationship marketing: Theory, methods and applications.* Atlanta: Emory University.

Sterne, L. W., & El Ansary, A. I. (1992). *Marketing channels.* Englewood Cliffs, NJ: Prentice Hall.

Stoltman, J., Tapp, S., & Lapidus, R. (1989). An examination of shopping scripts. In T. Srull (Ed.), *Advances for consumer research* (Vol. 16, pp. 384–391). Provo, UT: Association for Consumer Research.

Swan, J., & Trawick, I. (1981). Disconfirmation of expectation and satisfaction: A new concept. *Journal of Retailing, 5*(3), 49–67.

Tähtinen, J., & Blois, K. J. (2011). The involvement and influence of emotions in problematic business relationships. *Industrial Marketing Management, 40*(6), 907–918.

Tansik, D., & Smith, W. (1991). Dimension of job scripting in services organization. *International Journal of Service Industry Management, 2*(1), 35–49.

Thibaut, J. W., & Kelley, H. H. (1959). *The social psychology of groups.* New York, NY: Wiley.

Tsai, S. P. (2005). Integrated marketing as management of holistic consumer experience. *Business Horizons, 48*(5), 431–441.

Tse, D. K., & Wilton, P. C. (1988). Models of consumer satisfaction formation: An extension. *Journal of marketing research*, 204–212.

Tse, D. K., Nicosia, F., & Wilton, P. C. (1991). Consumer satisfaction as a process. *Psychology and Marketing, 7*(Fall), 177–193.

Tse, D. K., & Wilson, P. C. (1988). Model of consumer satisfaction formation: An extension. *Journal of Marketing Research, 25*(May), 204–212.

Tucker, W. (1964). The development of brand loyalty. *Journal of Marketing Research, 1*(August), 32–35.

Tuckman, B. W. (1965). Developmental sequence in small groups. *Psychological Bullettin, 63*, 384–399.

Hsieh, A. T., & Li, C. K. (2008). The moderating effect of brand image on public relations perception and customer loyalty. Marketing Intelligence & Planning, *26*(1), 26–42.

Van Heerde, H., & Bijmolt, T. H. A. (2005). Decomposing the promotional revenue bump for loyalty program members versus nonmembers. *Journal of Marketing Research, 42*(October), 443–457.

Verhees, F. J. H. M., Meulenberg, M. T. G., & Pennings, J. M. E. (2010). Performance expectations of small firms considering radical product innovation. *Journal of Business Research, 63*(7), 772–777.

Vrontis, D., & Thrassou, A. (2007). A new conceptual framework for business-consumer relationships. *Marketing Intelligence & Planning, 25*(7), 789–806.

Webster, F. E. (1994a). Defining the new marketing concept. *Marketing Management, 2*(4), 23–31.

Webster, F. E. (1994b). *Market-driven management: Using the new marketing concept to create a customer oriented company.* New York, NY: Wiley.

Wernerfelt, B. (1985). Brand loyalty and user skills. *Journal of Economic Behavior and Organization, 6*(December), 381–385.

Westbrook, R. A. (1987). Product/consumption-based affective responses and postpurschase processes. *Journal of Marketing Research, 24*(August), 258–270.

Williamson, O. (1975). *Markets and hierarchies: Analysis and antitrust implications.* New York: The Free Press.

Wind, Y. (1977). Brand loyalty and vulnerability. In A. G. Woodside, J. N. Sheth, & P. D. Bennet (Eds.), *Consumer and industrial buying behavior.* New York, NY: North Holland.

Woofford, J. (1994). An examination of the cognitive process used to handle employee job problems. *Academy of Management Journal, 37*(1), 180–192.

Yi, Y. (1990). A critical review of consumer satisfaction. In V. Zeithaml (Ed.), *Review of marketing* (pp. 68–123). Chicago: American Marketing Association.

Yim, C. K. B., Tse, D. K., & Chan, K. W. (2008). Strengthening customer loyalty through intimacy and passion: Roles of customer–firm affection and customer–staff relationships in services. *Journal of Marketing Research, 45*(6), 741–756.

Zeithaml, V. (1981). How consumer evaluation processes differ between goods and services. In J. Donnelly & W. George (Eds.), *Marketing of services* (pp. 186–200). Chicago: AMA.

Zeithaml, V. A., Parasuraman, A., & Berry, L. L. (1985). Problems and strategies in services marketing. *The Journal of Marketing*, 33–46.

Zeithaml, V., & Bitner, M. J. (1996). *Services marketing.* New York: McGraw-Hill.

Zhang, B., & He, C. (2012). Online customer loyalty improvement: Based on TAM psychological perception and loyal behavior model. *Advances in Information Technology and Management, 1*, 162–165.

Zohar, D., & Luria, G. (2003). Organizational meta-scripts as source of high reliability: The case of an army Armored Brigade. *Journal of Organizational Behavior, 24*(7), 837–859.

CHAPTER 3

A Model of Customer Retention in Business-Intensive Markets

3.1 The Determinants of Loyalty in a Digital Economy

At the dawn of e-commerce, there was a common feeling that it was senseless to talk about loyalty: it was believed that with the Internet, the ease of switching from one shop to another, and the opportunity to explore purchase alternatives in a very short time worldwide, would have discouraged any attempt by businesses to implement an e-loyalty strategy (Chen & Hitt, 2000; Jones, Motherbaugh & Beatty, 2000; Xu, Goedegebuure, & van der Heijden, 2006). Such a belief, however, was challenged by empirical evidence that Internet users visit their virtual stores much more often than any other traditional store (Inman, Winer, & Ferraro, 2009; Kaltcheva & Weitz, 2006; Adam, Dogramaci, Gangopadhyay & Yesha, 1999; Agrawal, Arjona & Lemmens, 2001; Allen, Kania & Yaeckel, 1998; Amit & Zott, 2001; Anderson, 2002; Bakos, 1997; Cameron, 1999; Brynjolfsson & Smith, 2000; Zwass, 1998). Moreover, the real explosion of e-commerce during the early years of the new economy led Internet companies to not deal at first with customer loyalty. Today, the situation of online markets is quite different: strong competition on the Web has encouraged businesses to take on a more critical and rational analysis of Internet marketing strategies, coming to the conclusion that in order to make a profit, traffic generation is not sufficient. Unlike the early diffusion of Internet technology, the success of a website does not depend on the number of visits but essentially on the frequency of use and its

M. Del Giudice, M.R. Della Peruta, *The Satisfaction of Change*,
DOI 10.1007/978-3-319-41884-1_3

ability to "retain" customers, minimizing the churn rate (Shankar, Smith, & Rangaswamy, 2003; Zhang & He, 2012). The model developed in this study focuses, as anticipated, on business-to-business (B2B) online customer experience, empirically testing the resistance to change of a typically unloyal business customer, consistently with the possession of a shopping script induced by the supplier. Instrumental to this model is the definition of online loyalty (e-loyalty); as in offline markets, loyalty has a dual nature, behavioral and cognitive, this is also true in the case of e-loyalty (online loyalty), the two dimensions of which are kept strictly separate: e-retention and e-fidelity. The former concerns the inertial forms of loyalty, that is, repeated purchasing behavior somehow forced and not accompanied by an adequate satisfaction and emotional involvement. Thus, e-retention indicates the pure and simple behavioral aspect of loyalty that, only if combined with adequate mental fidelity (e-fidelity), turns into e-loyalty. The inertial forms of loyalty are represented by all those cases in which a customer is forced to stay on a certain website because of:

- the high level of switching costs;
- the lack of presence or absence of competition.

Furthermore, on the Web, it is not likely for one to think that there are areas where competition is low: the strong acceleration of the imitative process in the net economy has gradually canceled any possibility of acting in a monopoly or oligopoly (or resorting to niche marketing strategies), except for very short periods of time. The other component of e-loyalty is, instead, e-fidelity, an exclusively mental and affective type of fidelity not accompanied by a corresponding repurchase behavior. E-fidelity is a key variable underlying most of the e-loyalty strategies. Thus, customer satisfaction holds the balance of power (Chung et al. 2007). Customer buying behavior is therefore primarily based on the ability of a company through its website (in the absence of a salesperson, as it occurs in offline markets) to make a shopping expedition satisfactory, engendering trust and loyalty, a perception of fairness in the relationship, and a desire to repurchase (Costabile, 2001; Shankar et al., 2003; Zhang & He, 2012). Thus, in this view, the online company would participate, through elements of its website, to the induction and creation of a customer's shopping script.

Although it is easier to activate a switching behavior moving to competitors with a simple click, a loyal online customer develops a type of loyalty that can be compared to Jacoby and Chestnut's true loyalty (1978),

Costabile's loyalty (2001), or Oliver's proactive loyalty (1997). In this sense, e-loyalty would be a particularly advanced form of loyalty that relates both cognitive and affective elements (e-fidelity), and behavioral elements (e-retention). The evidence of managerial studies on the subject confirms that a customer, after analyzing the possible purchase alternatives, tends to settle on a particular website. The competition to secure visibility and customers on the network becomes more and more aggressive (Moe & Yang, 2009; Schwartz, 2000), and such a trend is already evident in the search engines, where the nine major portals (AltaVista, AOL, Excite, Infoseek, Lycos, Microsoft, Netscape, Snap, and Yahoo) gather more than 90 percent of the traffic toward the Internet (Schwartz, 2000). Thus, in perspective, only the strongest websites will be able to survive and achieve loyal customers, provided that they use advanced customer loyalty techniques. In recent years, there has been a tendency in the literature to move from a profit-based management to a management in which loyalty is seen as a critical factor of success (Reichheld, 1996; Srinivasan & Hanssens, 2009; Villanueva & Hanssens, 2007). The main reasons that lead entrepreneurs to focus on customer loyalty (Bonfanti, Del Giudice & Papa, 2015) are:

- the high costs of acquiring new customers[1];
- customers' spending increases more than proportionally to the lengthening of the relationship[2];
- customer management costs decrease over time[3];
- loyal customers implement a positive word of mouth[4];
- loyal customers tolerate a premium price.[5]

3.2 Choices Made When Planning a Research Design: The Structural Features of the B2B Sector

The objective of this study is the empirical testing of the research hypotheses in the computing market, particularly in the B2B sector. This sector requires a different analysis approach than the business-to-customer (B2C) sector (on which the majority of empirical marketing research has focused).

One of the main differences between the two sectors, which is of great importance for the analysis of customer service tools (susceptible to induce the creation of a customer's shopping script), primarily consists of the number and type of buyers (Fill, 1999; Tidd & Bessant, 2009). In the market of online businesses, buyers tend to be less numerous but larger in size (Hamill & Gregory, 1997; Hutt & Speh, 2012; Mougayer, 1998). First of all, this implies that, since there are fewer buyers, the visibility of suppliers is more pronounced. It is therefore less important to use the website as a promotional tool (advertising banners, presence on search engines, and web promotion are secondary compared with the needs of brands in the consumer market) (Selden & MacMillan, 2006; Tsai, 2005; Vrontis & Thrassou, 2007). Of course, B2B suppliers that can rely on a wider base of potential customers (as it often occurs in the hi-tech, telecommunications, and information technology markets) tend to use web promotion techniques that more closely resemble those of the retail market (Baker, 1998; Le Meunier-FitzHugh & Lane, 2009; Quelch & Klein, 1996). Another key difference with the B2C sector is the size (in terms of structure, turnover, and volume of purchases) of the average customer: this implies, as an immediate consequence, a greater bargaining power for business customers. Therefore, it becomes essential for a supplier to try to thoroughly understand the needs of a business customer and how to fulfill them through the website (continuous purchasing, higher volumes, and customized supply conditions make the website of a wholesaler/distributor completely different, in its structural features and tools available, from that of a value-added reseller [VAR] or a dealer).[6] Moreover, the downside is that in the business market, there can also be a limited number of suppliers (as in some areas of job order production).[7]

The typical low number detectable in these areas is of considerable importance for marketing and the support of customer retention: the need for external information by suppliers leads them to publish on their website information about new contracts and products, in addition to testimonies provided by existing customers (Lee, Huang, Barnes, & Kao, 2010; Turnbull, 1999). Since this information is of great importance also for competitors, a common feature of all B2B websites is recognized access (subject to prior registration) by customers or potential buyers: through the website, B2B suppliers have the opportunity to learn more about their customers and develop a differential marketing aimed at stimulating retention processes. However, for the purposes of this study, what matters most is the nature of the buying process: as pointed out, research is focused indeed on the creation of a shopping script induced by the online supplier's customer service, and its impact on the customer's resistance to change (Baker, 1998; Seybold, 1999; Turnbull, 1999). Thus, business purchases involve a more complex decision-making process than that of consumers (Webster & Wind, 1996).[8] Therefore, the website's contents should be designed to serve the different needs of the different members of the business customer's purchase team (Masanell & Ricart 2010; McGrath, 2010; Poon & Jevons, 1997; Srinivasan, Anderson, & Ponnavolu, 2002). Furthermore, the website must make the shopping process simple and straightforward, offering customized content to its users, to the people who influence the purchase, and to those who actively decide. And if the buyer and the decision-maker are the same person, as it occurs in small- and medium-sized enterprises (SMEs), the shopping script should be as straightforward and simple as possible to encourage repeated purchases. Of course, the layout and web architecture design should take into account consumer needs as much as possible, in order to guide web marketing policies accordingly (Kotler et al., 2009; O'Sullivan, 2010).

The type of purchase, and consequently the shopping script, can vary significantly according to the industry of reference: for example, companies that produce goods on order will receive high unit value but low-volume orders, whereas companies that produce consumer goods will receive high-volume but low unit value orders. In the first case, it is unlikely that the Internet is used for the actual transaction, which requires a special contract and complex preliminary agreements. In the second case, instead, the orders involve large volumes consistent with low unit values: therefore, e-commerce transactions will be more appropriate and the Internet can offer several advantages over traditional methods of purchase (such as mail or fax orders).[9] Moreover, the decision to purchase goods and technical services for businesses will be more complex and require more time than for products intended for consumers (Turnbull, 1999; Webster & Wind, 1996), and the time required to choose a supplier and evaluate the product may be much longer.[10]

Finally, between the B2B and B2C markets, there are structural differences in communication, which are found in the design and architecture of the websites and, therefore, have a direct impact on the creation and learning of the customer's shopping script (and consequently, directly affect the customer's resistance to change) (Lee & Kim, 2008). There is widespread evidence of this in the literature: for example, Brougaletta (1985) and Gilliand and Johnston (1997) analyzed the differences between business-oriented and consumer-oriented marketing communication. Fill (1999), for his part, summarized the differences:

1. in a B2B context, the composition of the communication mix is different: advertising and sales promotion tend to be a support for personal sales;
2. below-the-line techniques tend to be more common than above-the-line ones;
3. the products intended for businesses tend to involve a greater effort since the level of specialization and degree of customer information are higher.

Moreover, with regard to the creation of a B2B shopping script, in the literature, Patricia Seybold's suggestions are a useful reference (1999).[11] The US analyst focuses in particular on a few guiding principles, possible critical factors of success in the implementation of an Internet strategy that points to customer retention through the creation of a shopping script. Among these, the simplification of the processes that impact customers is above all of particular interest: Seybold (1999) cites the example of FedEx, which used the Internet to modernize the service offered to customers, by simplifying and networking order, tracking, and payment procedures.

It is also important to provide a complete view of customer relationship: this can be done through a theoretical study of the customer's needs and preferences shown in purchases (through the analysis of cookies and log files, and with the support of data mining and web mining). Similarly, another key factor is the ability to speed up the decision-making process and reduce shopping expedition time: the learning of a shopping script by a customer gives it the possibility to conclude purchases more rapidly, orienting its competitive advantage over other companies in the industry, precisely on time-based competition. However, the tools available to suppliers to reduce churn and boost retention are still many: in the literature, it is of considerable importance, for example, to focus on providing customers with the information, often technical, they need to do their business.

The features of the B2B market highlighted so far, and the typical style of the shopping process of its actors, compared with what occurs in consumer markets, have made them more difficult to be thoroughly understood by the in-depth analysis of the management literature (Kotler, Armstrong, Saunders, & Wong, 2008). However, this study has chosen just this sector as a point of reference, because, for the features of its actors and their decision-making processes, it allows a more detailed and complete study of the variables that have an impact on customer loyalty. A firm makes its purchases in a case of limited emotionality and high rationality: professional buyers are usually considerably more informed than average end users; hence, they are much more demanding than the latter.

Thus, if, on the one hand, it is difficult to turn them into loyal customers, on the other hand, compared with actors in a B2C market, they are more prone to learn a shopping script. In fact, the repetition and continuity of their purchases allow the supplier to work more on the creation of a customer's shopping script, which can have a direct impact on his resistance to change. Unlike an "individual" customer (B2C market), whose purchases can be random events, a "business" customer (B2B market) is characterized by a strong rationality in its decision-making process, resulting from the periodic repetition of purchases and the handling of higher volumes of goods. Its purchases, compared with the former, are not the manifestation of an often personal need, but intended for an exclusively professional activity.

This urges business customers to think in terms of profit maximization, focusing on the optimization of the acquisition costs of the products to be allocated to the core of their business. It is easy to understand that with similar conditions a "business" customer will tend to be more disloyal, in a digital economy, than an "individual" customer, because it will give more weight to the rationality of its choices, rather than the emotionality of its needs. For the purpose of this study, it was therefore intuitive to assume that for such a customer, the resistance to change may just result from the presence of a shopping script that optimizes its decision-making process[12] and minimizes shopping expedition time. Thus, it is equally intuitive to understand the choice of conducting an empirical verification precisely in this sector. Similarly, to verify the proposed model of customer retention, it was decided to set the empirical investigation in one of the industries the most similar to the competitive markets described by Bertrand (and hence more liable to customer disloyalty): the market of computing products, typically characterized by a pulverization of the offer, perfect substitutability of many brands, almost perfect price transparency, limited presence of information asymmetries, and rapid technical product obsolescence.

The choice, confirmed by several indications derived from the management literature and marketing research (Brown & Eisenhardt, 1997; Iansiti & West, 1997; Prandelli, Sahweney, & Verona, 2008; Sawney & Prandelli, 2000), is the most critical point of the research design. In fact, digital markets provide a number of opportunities for the investigation and verification of the concept of customer retention, but the need to study customer resistance to change, and its possible inductive factors, has led our empirical analysis to a typically higher churn rate context (Sawney & Prandelli, 2000; Srinivasan et al., 2002). In fact, the validation of the developed model assumes a meaning that is scientifically more conclusive because it has been carried out in such a complex competitive scenario. However, at this point in the discussion, it is necessary to highlight the features of the B2B website susceptible to create a customer's shopping script. A website with a high level of customer service, thanks to the presence of numerous tools, preferential pathways, collaborative masks, etc., will more easily direct the customer in its shopping expedition, making it acquire a specific behavior at the time of purchase, which can be typically found in the shopping script (Sterne, 2000: Sterne, 2010)). The developed research design, the subject of the empirical verification presented in the next chapter, includes the study of the importance of the possession of this script recognized by the customer itself through the manifestation of a spontaneous resistance to change its supplier (nonswitching behavior). This voluntary resistance will be tested through the verification of the hypothetical correlation between the knowledge of the shopping script and the recognition of switching costs when abandoning the script itself. At this point in the discussion, it becomes fundamental to understand what structural elements of the B2B website induce the creation of such a shopping script (Bruggen, Foubert, & Gremler, 2011; Hsu & Chiang 2011; Jacobs & De Klerk, 2010). The examination of the model will be conducted through the analysis of:

- the cognitive processes for the emergence of the business customer script;
- the information from the business customer required to define the shopping script;
- the tools available to the supplier to integrate and manage the shopping script.

3.3 The Emergence of Client Scripts: Latent Cognitive Processes

For the purpose of this study, it is necessary first of all to show the latent cognitive processes underlying the creation of the concept of business customer script (Del Giudice, Della Peruta & Maggioni, 2013). As reported in the literature (Shapiro & Varian, 1999; Smith, 2006; Srinivasan et al., 2002), particular relevance is assigned to processes that determine:

- the consumers' tendency to express some cognitive inertia, that is, to seek confirmation to what has already been the object of experience (selection processes) (Costabile, 2001; Smith, 2006);
- the production of information capable of guiding purchase/consumption choices and user experience (association processes) (Lee & Kim, 2008);
- the organization of this information to assess, *ex ante* and *ex post*, the value and utility generated by the selected product/service (evaluation processes) (Lechner & Kreutzer, 2010).

3.3.1 Selection Processes

Selection processes are aimed at preserving the constructs of preexisting knowledge and, in particular, the attitudes developed by a business customer toward the relationship (Costabile, 2001). They can be classically broken down into three major components:

1. the cognitive component, concerning the knowledge and beliefs of the business customer;
2. the affective component, which relates to the sphere of emotions and values (enhanced in the B2C sector, but rather limited, in this case, since customers belong to the B2B sector);
3. the pragmatic component, which results in established behavioral orientations (particularly strong, given the characteristics of the decision-making process and the rationality of the business customer script).

Each component, in turn, is characterized by a certain degree of complexity, and by a set of positive or negative values arising from a customer's well-rooted beliefs; the intensity of these values is, of course, an indicator of the resistance to change of the various components (Costabile, 2001; Smith, 2006). The stability of a given attitude is therefore dependent on the existence of a double consonance: at a global level, between the components of cognitive, affective, and pragmatic nature, and at the disaggregate level, between the values associated with each component. Selection processes aimed at avoiding situations of imbalance due to a dissonance among the cognitive, affective, and pragmatic components that define the structure of attitudes are based on the activation of mechanisms of:

- *selective exposure and attention* to data that is consistent with expectations derived from possessed knowledge and previous choices;
- *selective understanding* of data, that is, attribution to the data itself of a meaning consistent with existing cognitive schemas;
- *selective retention* of data that is able to provide information aligned with the established system of values, beliefs, and attitudes.

Essentially, the mechanisms of the first type govern the perception of data relating to products which, once encoded, access the customer's primary memory; the mechanisms of the second type, instead, govern the interpretation of the data and its translation into information, which, through the mechanisms of the third type, are internalized in the secondary memory (Alba et al., 1997). In the company's view, understanding the described mechanisms is crucial to build and increase customer loyalty, which, as a resource of trust, feeds on information that is able to validate the cognitive schemas produced by the customer (Alba et al., 1997). In fact, the perception taken up by a specific brand or sign in the cognitive system of a business customer is also influenced by the supplier's ability to reassure it continuously on the validity of the choice made, avoiding the birth of dissonant information, induced by the communications of rival operators or by user experiences which do not comply with the expectations (Shostak, 1977). This is of crucial importance, because, if the number or quality of this information is likely to force to change the cognitive schema previously adopted, the change is radical and trust will be compromised (Wells & Foxall, 2012).

3.3.2 Association Processes

Through association processes, customers define the network of mental associations between the features of products and services and their sphere of values (Agarwal & Karahanna, 2000; Alba & Hasher, 1983; Costabile, 2001; Schank & Abelson, 1977). To understand how this type of processes works, the means-end chain model is particularly relevant. It reconnects the content of these associations to three levels of abstraction, each preliminary to the following, represented by:

- the attributes of the offer;
- the benefits provided by the product or service;
- individual values.

The attributes of the offer can be divided into denotative and connotative; the first refer to tangible features and are generally related to the expectations about the technical and functional performance of the products or services, while the latter relate to intangible features, related to further (emotional and psychological) meaning that a customer attaches to the objects of purchase, going beyond their usage functions (Sterne, 1999).

The benefits provided by the product or service can be classified, instead, along two fundamental dimensions, respectively, the type of advantages sought and the ability (or willingness) of the customer to specify himself the nature of these advantages.

The first dimension allows to differentiate the benefits of a functional nature, closely related to the performance of the good or service, from the benefits of a psychological and social nature, primarily related to the meaning adopted on a symbolic level (Rischkowsky & Döring, 2008). This dichotomy is primarily reflected on the relative importance that the characteristics of the offer may take in the evaluation processes; in fact, if the research of benefits of a functional nature prevails, it is likely that the rationality of choice emphasizes the role played by denotative attributes, capable of influencing the quality/price ratio of the offer system. In the opposite case, instead, the centrality of connotative attributes increases, with particular reference to the symbolic and fiduciary meaning held by the brand and company image. The prevalence of symbolic benefits makes it very difficult for a firm to control the evaluations following a purchase, which underlies the level of satisfaction perceived by a customer, and hence customer loyalty (Costabile, 2001). Second, the suggested differentiation affects the importance a customer attaches to fundamental types of channels and information stimuli designed to intervene in the creation of preferences, and thus in the content of the communications enabled by the company to properly orient customer expectations. For example, the desire to prove the membership of a particular social group, or the originality of a lifestyle, through possessions or the attendance of certain stores, highlights the opportunity to mainly use emotional communication, designed to increase the psychological value of the acts of purchase and consumption.

The second dimension suggests the distinction between implicit and explicit benefits. The latter are associated with conscious motives, which, with no particular difficulties, can be identified by companies, and hence hardly underlie opportunities translatable in long-term competitive advantages; however, their satisfaction is the key to access the set of alternatives considered by customers, so they cannot be ignored. Implicit benefits, instead, appear to be related both to motives that the customer himself does not have complete knowledge of, and needs clearly perceived but not externalized, for psychological reasons (insecurity, conformity, fear of revealing hidden aspects of personality) or because they are conflicting with social conventions, role expectations, or codes of shared behavior. The third level of abstraction concerns the individual values and the associations related to the values evoked by the brand or sign. These can be defined as mental associations of important goals the customer wants to achieve in his life at the level of: (a) behavior and social status (instrumental external values); (b) self-esteem and the conditions of existence (terminal internal values). The former include social and economic status, competence, integrity, sociability; the latter, self-esteem, freedom, health, social harmony, personal satisfaction, safety, etc. In general, the prevalence of instrumental values related to appearance rather than existence directs customers to search for symbolic and ostentatious benefits, inducing them to base the purchasing process of products/services on attributes of a connotative nature. Therefore, the understanding of the association processes developed by customers proves to be very useful for the development of customer loyalty, which is essentially subject to the firm's ability to clarify to its customers the connections between denotative and connotative features of the product/service and the higher levels of the means-end chain (Phillips & Reynolds, 2009; Van Rekom & Wierenga, 2007).

3.3.3 Evaluation Processes

Through these processes, customers, based on the cognitive associations that represent possible offer alternatives and the information produced by user experience, finalize their shopping process, define the shopping script, and verify the validity of the choices they made (Bergen, Dutta, & Shugan, 1996). The main cognitive constructs underlying the processes of evaluation and elaboration of the shopping script are represented by subjective beliefs and objective criteria of choice (given, in our case, the customer service tools provided by the supplier's website). Their interaction leads to the creation of definite pre-sales attitudes, which in turn translate into specific expectations toward the goods and services subject to comparison, and purchasing decisions (as we have already seen in the analysis of the literature review, relatively to the contributions to the script theory) (Alba et al., 1997). The information resulting from the use of the selected offer alternative is retroactive relatively to beliefs and criteria, confirming or not these knowledge structures (the confirmation–disconfirmation paradigm discussed when dealing with the determinants of satisfaction) (Zhao, Lynch, & Chen, 2010). This feedback is embodied in the production of a post-purchase attitude; the comparison between this and the expectations underlies indeed the level of satisfaction perceived, possible resistance to change, and the willingness to reuse the shopping script, because it is a bearer of satisfactory results: and then finally, customer loyalty.

In the analysis of the evaluation processes, certain aspects are particularly important, and are related to the identification of:

- the determinants of the value perceived by a customer (in the purchase phase and following the consumption experience);
- their relative importance;
- the sequence of the fundamental cognitive constructs generated by the activities of comparison, selection, and use of goods and services (beliefs, attitudes, pre-purchase attitudes, perceived consonance between expectations and outcomes of the consumption experience, and post-purchase attitudes).

With regard to the value perceived by a customer, it is necessary to carry out an in-depth analysis of the perceptual system of consumers (Erasmus, Boshoff, & Rosseau, 2001). The associations a customer uses to differentiate the existing offer alternatives and the choices made in the definition of the script are based on precise tangible and intangible attributes, whose correlation with the benefits sought and the individual system of values orients the evaluation processes (Alba et al., 1997). In this regard, it is worth recalling that to properly manage customer loyalty, it is essential to consider the feedback effects from the use of the selected product. These effects can indeed change substantially both the composition of the set of features which are deemed relevant and the hierarchy of the selection criteria. In this study, resistance to change and consequently customer loyalty arise from the consideration of a more or less extensive set of design and architectural features of the website, and it is therefore unrealistic to ignore their interrelations. A separate analysis of the numerous evaluation parameters does not allow a firm to determine the effects that the increase (or decrease) of intensity of a certain attribute can have on the perceived value of the shopping script, and hence on the cognitive dimension of loyalty.

Preferences produced by the final definition of the script, in the presence of a confirmation of expectations acquired during purchasing, are therefore characterized by a substantial stability, which is further increased by the weight of the satisfaction inherent in the same script. In the light of the importance attached to a shopping script by a business customer, not only in psychological but especially in managerial terms, it is however very likely that phenomena of cognitive dissonance may occur, and their successful solution is subject to the birth of loyalty to the regular supplier and the prevention of switching behavior. Thus, customer choices become dependent on beliefs actively acquired while living the purchase script. In such circumstances, purchase problems induce business customers to adopt customary behavior, and they are due to the desire to simplify the shopping process, save time, and blend in this script the imperative of satisfaction.

3.4 Definition of *Shopping Script*: Information from Business Customers

At this point in the discussion, it is necessary to understand the mechanisms of development of the shopping script by a supplier and learning by a business customer. The former, in particular, will be based, as well as on the entrepreneur's experience, also and above all on a series of vital information derived from observation of the business customer.

Scripts are characterized by a common part in most customers (Schank & Abelson, 2013) , but also and above all, as we earlier saw in the literature review, by the presence of firm-specific elements that make the relationship between the supply company and the client company unique and unrepeatable: practically, a customized script (Johnson, Bellman, & Lohse, 2003; Simonson, 2005; Srinivasan et al., 2002; Wind & Rangaswamy, 1999). An example of such a perspective is given, in our field of study, by the one-to-one marketing developed by Internet companies through customer profiling. Proper customization of the client script has the advantage of a strong impact on e-fidelity, as reported in the literature (Srinivasan et al., 2002).

The objectives in developing a customized relationship, beyond the requirements linked to the definition of a unique script, are also connected to the creation of additional factors of resistance to change for business customers: if the latter, after developing an ongoing relationship with a supplier, decided to change, it would face the problem of a cold start (Johnson et al., 2003; Srinivasan et al., 2002). That would mean moving from a situation where everything is known, where the company has gathered a large amount of information, to a new situation that requires a commitment to provide personal information and a certain time for the company to build a reliable profiling. This means that, as time goes by, the improvement and the constant refinement of profiling will discourage the user to abandon the website, both because it would lose all the benefits of *being known* and because of the practical problem of having to waste a great deal of time to provide again its data to the new website[13] (Lombardo, Kroonenberg, & D'Ambra, 2000; Mutula & van Brakel, 2006). The technological tools that allow effective customization of the website by providing targeted advice for each individual user, and systems that prevent information overload, are numerous. For the purpose of defining a shopping script, we shall here examine the technological tools that allow, on the one hand, to collect information from business customers, and on the other hand, to affect customization of the shopping script, finalizing all to a higher satisfaction of the customer itself (Ivan & Dickson, 2008).

3.4.1 Log Files

One of the unique features of Internet companies is the possibility of extracting information on the user from its web surfing (Edwards & Bauer, 2005). This feature is a strategic resource in the definition of a customized shopping script for a business customer. To achieve such a purpose, Internet companies manage data through a data warehouse.[14]

In order to define a shopping script and customize it, the traces left by a business customer on the supplier's server during every browsing session, which can be extracted from log files, may be numerous and of different types:

1. *Date and time of requests.* By knowing access timing, it is possible to schedule real-time initiatives on the website, anticipate any peak in the requests, and extrapolate the reading times of single pages for users identified by cookies or registration.

2. *URL of origin.* It is possible to know the websites previously visited by customers and visitors, and possibly insert advertising banners or links.
3. *Type and version of browser.* The browsers to be supported may be defined, making the shopping expedition faster and the shopping experience more satisfying.
4. *IP (Internet Protocol) address of the visitor.* Unlike the B2C sector, where ISPs use the Dynamic Host Configuration Protocol (DHCP) to assign addresses dynamically, business users often use static IP addresses uniquely identifying their presence on the website.
5. *Cookies sent by visitors.* Thanks to cookies that business customers have on their personal computers (PCs), it is possible to know what other competitor websites have been visited, and intervene promptly.
6. *Cookies sent by the server.* Data from one visit to another on a user's PC can be stored, thus allowing to simply outline a behavioral script for each customer (required for the definition of the shopping script).
7. *Query text inserted within the URL.*[15]
8. *Number of bytes transferred and received.* They give an idea of the time spent browsing the website.

3.4.2 Cookies

Another very useful tool to complement the analysis of log files in order to know the customer and customize its shopping script are cookies. They are text strings, usually of a negligible size, stored on the hard drive of the user's computer.[16] Cookies, if properly associated with a collection of personal data in a data warehouse can provide a very good support to the processes of customization on the Web.

There are different levels of use of cookies. The first level, completely anonymous, unrelated to any personal explicit information (registration form) or implicit (analysis of website browsing by a business customer), simply provides the opportunity to enable certain rules of penetration of advertising to a unique user: the rate of impressions (the number of times the same banner is exposed during a session), the clickthrough rate (number of times a banner is "clicked"), and the sequence in which more creativity may be displayed as part of the same campaign. A second level is related to database marketing with explicit information about the user (gathered, for example, through a registration form): based on this information, a company can identify precisely the subjects to which a particular banner may be shown, with specific social, demographic, and cultural profiles. In the end, a third and final level concerns the use of cookies as a means of improving browsing experience since a business customer is automatically recognized thanks to cookies: in this way, the website can directly "upload" the characteristics of its shopping script (by setting, for example, a customer profile, reserved discounts, shipping and billing addresses, methods of payment, etc.). Once the data has been collected, web companies need to extract information from the data warehouses, which may be useful to enrich user profiling and determine a more effective customization of the shopping script (Jacobs & De Klerk, 2010). For this purpose, statistical methodologies known as KDD (knowledge discovery in databases) are involved.

3.4.3 *Knowledge Discovery in Databases and Data Mining*

Knowledge discovery in databases[17, 18] is an interactive process of information extraction from databases (Mili, Benzarti, Meurs, Obaid, Gonzalez-Huerta, Haj-Salem & Boubaker, 2016; Lombardo et al., 2000). The process takes raw data as input and provides useful information as output, which is the result of subsequent processing phases (Anderberg, 1973; Giudici, 2003). The process of data extraction for the definition of a shopping script begins with the selection phase. Raw data are segmented and selected according to some guidelines.[19] After selecting the desired data, obviously, it is not necessary to analyze the entire content in order to identify useful information. Under certain conditions and for certain types of data mining operations, it may be more appropriate firstly to extract a sample of the data and, then, to explore it: we then move on to the pre-processing phase.[20] In this phase, data cleaning is performed to eliminate possible errors, and decisions are made on how to deal with missing data (data integration). After selection and identification, the data is processed to ensure navigability and usability (Córdoba-Pachón, Pilkington, & Bernroider, 2012). Such an objective is pursued both by converting one type of data into another (nominal values into numeric in the case of subsequent use of neural networks), and defining new types, derived from processing attributes (applying mathematical or logical operators) (transformation phase). Furthermore, the data is reconfigured to ensure it is "significant". The patterns identified and extracted from the system are used as a decisional support for analysts or managers. Thus, the purpose of

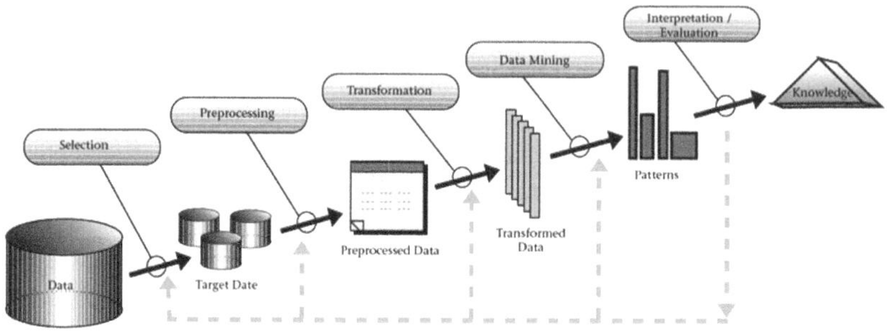

Fig. 3.1 The process of knowledge discovery in databases

the result of the interpretation is not only to display (graphically or logically) the output of data mining, but also to filter the information to be presented (interpretation and evaluation phases) (Fig. 3.1).

3.4.4 Data Mining

In between the phases of transformation and interpretation of the data is data mining, a process of extraction of knowledge from large databases through the use of algorithms that detect associations "hidden" within the information, and make them visible. The expression "data mining" groups together various data mining techniques for data exploration, all with the aim of identifying the most important information and making it available and directly usable for the analysis of customer behavior and the creation of a customized shopping script (Kroonenberg, 2008; Lombardo et al., 2000). For web companies, the techniques in question have the advantage of being able to identify hidden information from the data possessed. This means that user profiling can be constantly improved, and it is possible to understand more thoroughly the customized content to offer to business customers. The managerial importance of such an operation is straightforward: the competitive dynamism of B2B digital markets involves constant monitoring of the behavior of business customers. It is therefore essential to rely on a fast and efficient information system, especially in view that the system should provide the company with vital information for the redefinition of the scripts and the reorganization of customer service (Han & Kamber, 2007).[21]

The major data mining techniques can be classified as:

- *classification*;
- *clustering*;
- *regression*;
- *summarization*;
- *dependency modeling*;
- *association rules*;
- *sequential patterns*.

For the purposes of this study and the research hypotheses developed, it is worth to focus here on the techniques (association rules and sequential patterns) that have most immediate applications for the behavioral analysis of business customers, and thus have a greater relevance for the determination of the shopping script.

3.4.4.1 Association Rules

Association rules[22] are a technique widely used to decide what will be the content of the website to be offered to users. An application of this technique in web mining is, for example, the detection of the correlation of accesses to different files by a certain user. Based on the behavior of other users, it is possible to anticipate what will be its behavior and provide personalized advice (or “calibrate” differently the tools that will characterize the business customer’s shopping script). Using association rules technique, it is possible, for example, to highlight correlations as follows:

- 60 % of customers that accessed the page/company/products/ also visited the page/company/products/product1.html
- 40 % of customers that accessed the page/company/products/product1.html also visited the page /company/products/product2.html
- 30 % of customers that accessed the page company/special-offers.html made an online purchase in /company/products/product1.html

In web mining, thanks to the hierarchical structure of websites, such techniques are also useful for reducing the search field of association rules (e.g. if support for the company/product is low, it can be concluded that there are no significant associations between sub-pages with the URLs company/products/product1.html and company/products/product2.html, even if there is an adequate support between them) (Sénécal, Fredette, Léger, Courtemanche & Riedl, 2015).

3.4.4.2 Sequential Patterns

Sequential patterns[23] are, instead, an evolution of Associations Rules. They are probably the most effective tool available to suppliers to analyze a shopping script and formulate important corrective hypotheses (thanks to this technique, in fact, Internet companies can analyze a user's past behavior and provide an even more effective customization) (Wicks, 1992).

The inputs of the technical analysis of the script in question provide:

- a set of sequences known as "data sequences" (which represent the different steps of a shopping script);
- a time window (the interval of time within which the episodes that form the shopping script are to be found);
- a threshold rate (able to determine when the episodes are significant).

Of course, the output is represented by the sequential patterns. By analyzing the information from the logs stored in the server's memory for a certain period, time relationships can be determined as follows:

- 30 % of customers that visited the page company/products/product1.html made a search on Yahoo! using the keywords W1 and W2 over a period of two weeks;
- 60 % of customers that made an online order in company/products/product1.html also made an order in company1/products/product4.html in the last 15 days.

All this allows to "calibrate" the customer service and the tools of a website according, precisely, to the behavioral script of a business (Balasubramanian, Raghunathan & Mahajan, 2005; Taylor, Cronin & Hansen, 1991).

3.4.5 The Output Phase: Website Customization According to the Resulting Shopping Script

At this point, the company has at its disposal all the necessary information to customize its website according to the firm-specific shopping script of its business customer. The literature upholds the theory that a company may exploit the information of individual users (information filtering) or may combine the different information on the users to give more effective browsing advice (collaborative filtering) (Soto-Acosta, Casado-Lumbreras & Cabezas-Isla, 2010); Soto-Acosta, Popa & Palacios-Marqués, 2015). The tools that, on the basis of the information obtained by the customer, allow to intervene in order to optimize the shopping scripts are the recommender systems.[24] These systems allow to build a sort of virtual store tailored to each individual user of the website: of course, this unique feature will fall within the more general shopping script of the business customer. There are different options to achieve effective recommender systems. The first is called information filtering[25] and is based on building a user profile that allows to give advice and anticipate the user's wishes. The information overload is nowadays one of the greatest threats that can undermine the definition of a shopping script; the latter, instead, must be immediate and ensure that the shopping expedition of a business customer is rapid and efficient. To overcome such a problem, Internet companies have developed effective filtering tools so that only relevant and interesting information may reach the user. Many of the current filtering systems are based on the construction of behavioral heuristics: they try to extract characteristics from the observation of customer behavior in order to predict which information should be selected and which not. A more simple methodology that is widely used is, instead, collaborative filtering, which bases its logic on the word of mouth. A user receives advice from people who have similar tastes and bought the same products. All the information collected about the users is combined so to create clusters in which the different users who connect to the website can be placed and give proper advice.[26] Through the collaborative filtering technique, it is possible to combine information possessed by different users in order to give useful and targeted advice[27] (Liberati, C., & Camillo, 2014).

3.4.6 Web Mining for Website Customization

Through web mining techniques, it is possible to understand how users view a company's website. The managerial relevance of the tool is straightforward: in the sector in question, business customers can initially define a customer's shopping script that is not fully satisfying. Thanks to web mining, companies can avail themselves of a powerful tool to monitor the efficiency of their website in real time. As a direct result, in the event of a decline in the positive perceptions of the website by a business customer, an event that would jeopardize its resistance to change, the supplier company can rapidly make all necessary steps to strengthen the user's customer satisfaction by redefining online customer service tools, the protagonists of the shopping expedition.

Website design errors are one of the decisive variables of customer detection: in a competitive scenario where the time factor is a critical resource, the issues of website usability (Nielsen, 2000; Nielsen & Tahir, 2002), interface design (Del Giudice, 2004; Nielsen, 2000; Polski & Del Giudice, 2004), and the low level of customer service tools and templates that simplify the shopping expedition and contribute to the definition of the script, or long download time of web pages, can irreparably undermine retention (Nielsen, 2000; Nielsen & Tahir, 2002). Of course, the shortcomings of a website can be monitored thanks to a plethora of analyses addressed to the observation of user behavior (Nielsen & Loranger, 2006). The analyses ideally conductive to monitor and optimize the effectiveness of the shopping scripts defined by business customers are:

- *analysis of the general trend* (a quantitative analysis with the purpose of evaluating the success or failure of a website and of web promotion strategies);
- *analysis of website content* (the information provided is critical to understand what topics, including those presented, are the most popular with visitors. The ability to provide good-quality content and the possibility of downloading white papers are, in our opinion, one of the key variables that have an impact on user loyalty);
- *link analysis*;
- *path analysis*.

3.5 Definition of *Shopping Script*: Tools Available to Suppliers to Integrate and Manage *Shopping Scripts*

In the previous sections, the issue of defining a shopping script based on the information from a business customer, and on the Internet technologies designed for collection and reprocessing, has been discussed. The problems related to the definition of shopping scripts are widely attributable to the problem of the influence of the environment on the behavior of individuals. In marketing, Werner (1985) was among the first scholars to introduce the concept of "scenario", referring to service encounter. Similarly, the issue is relatable, with reference to offline markets, to the relationships between customers and contact staff (in our study, the website takes the place of the salesperson): in this view, the contributions by

Price, Arnould, and Tierney (1995), Tzafrir and Gur (2007), and Yee, Yeung, and Cheng (2009) provide interesting insights about the role exerted by the environment on the relationship between the actors of the shopping process. From this perspective, the definition of shopping script can be seen as a meeting point between the elaboration of the information derived from observation of the customer's buying behavior and search for additional points of contact between the customer and the supplier. In a business-intensive context such as the one chosen for this study, these contact points are aimed at optimizing the relationship with the customer, investigating more thoroughly its shopping script and creating additional factors that stimulate its resistance to change. The tools developed by web companies for these purposes are commonly referred to in the literature as "listening tools". The main listening tool is the call center. The new digital technologies have marked the transition from an idea of simple helpline, aimed at solving customer issues, to a real tool of customer interaction.

3.5.1 Web Call Centers

The convergence of information technology and the increasingly wide diffusion of the Internet as a universal means of communication among businesses has rapidly transformed the technology and purpose of call centers. The development of web call centers or web contact centers allows to add to inbound and outbound functionality typical of call centers also multimedia functions (Nielsen, 2000). Web call centers work so that if a business customer, while visiting the supplier's website, needs vocal assistance, it has to press a button to activate a gateway that starts a paid or toll-free phone call to the supplier's call center, at which point the gateway connects the agent with the user via the IP network (Nielsen & Tahir, 2002). Web call centers allow the connection between an informational web and a telephone operator in order to assist the user while browsing and give advice. It can be immediately seen that, for a customer that has not yet fully defined its shopping script, "physical" intervention by the company can be decisive. Just in order to develop these interactions, many B2B websites give the option to subscribe to specific services, through which a business customer can access the voice connection with an operator by clicking on an icon (Sterne, 2000). From that moment, they will be able to talk, surf the Internet at the same time (web collaboration), share the same screen, and, if necessary, the operator will be able to send web pages of interest to the customer's PC (web page pushing). In fact, thanks to co-browsing, user and operator synchronize the web pages and share the same files, utilizing the same telephone line used for surfing (it is also possible to start visual interaction by exchanging images through video web contact center systems).

The positive impact that the possibility for a user to interact with a voice operator can have on a company's business is moreover a data also highlighted by independent market research (Sterne, 2010). In fact, it can often happen that web surfers cannot find the information or the item they are searching for, or that they want to solve some doubts before possibly purchasing a product: these issues could be solved by providing a set of online relationship services with the customer, which may consist of not only voice or video interaction (web call centers or web video call centers), but also the exchange of text messages (text chats)[28] (Sterne, 2000).

3.5.2 *Text Chats*

Another tool to manage the interaction with business customers are text chats. At the beginning of their diffusion, Internet technologies were used to facilitate online point-to-point communication (Stephen, 2004; Molina, Campaña, & Ortega, 2016). Next-generation text chats allow to listen to customers and reduce service costs by allowing a significant reduction in the number of telephone lines, rates, and operators required to manage the phone calls. Chats are a free option for customers that provide immediate access to the products and services of a company. Realistically, it is possible to manage a maximum of two or three chats simultaneously as a greater number would require to spend too much time online due to extended chat pauses. Text chats help to increase customer satisfaction as each call lasts on average four minutes less than a normal phonecall, and it has also been proved that many users prefer chats to phone calls because they avoid oral communication.

3.6 Tools Available to Firms to Monitor the Evolution of Shopping Scripts

3.6.1 *Virtual Communities*

The competitive dynamics of the digital markets, especially in B2B, require constant monitoring of the shopping scripts created by consumers (Balasubramanian & Mahajan, 2001; Cummins, Peltier, Schibrowsky, & Nill, 2014). The evolution of shopping scripts can be monitored online by a company primarily through the analysis of virtual communities.[29] Virtual communities are a concept recently introduced on the Web: they allow individuals and businesses to interact using tools such as e-mails or newsgroups. In the literature, heated debates on virtual communities have alternated (Armstrong & Hagel, 1996), since they offer a unique opportunity for businesses to know more about their customers, without developing a one-to-one marketing. According to Hagel (1988), the great power of virtual communities lies in the "virtuous circles" they activate. Contents with a precise focus activate the entry of new members, which in turn tend to increase the quality and quantity of shared knowledge. As a community gradually expands, of course, the loyalty of its members increases, and obviously also the purchasing power of the participants is enhanced, since the growth of the forum attracts visits from more and more sellers. As the size and complexity of the community grows, its potential of data collection and profile construction gradually increases, thus allowing a marketing activity which is increasingly targeted. This positive cycle of actions and reactions gives birth to precious opportunities of relationship marketing for suppliers: communities are a primary source of information on customers and their shopping scripts (also on those possibly developed by competitors). Virtual communities also have the characteristic of promoting the transformation of the material economy, that is, that of mass production, into virtual economy, through effort and enhancement of communication and knowledge[30] (Kim, 2000).

3.6.2 Corporate Clubs

Another way to create groupings of users and monitor the evolution of the shopping scripts is to create corporate clubs. With the Web, for reasons related to ergonomics, effectiveness, and efficiency of the means of communication, the importance of these tools is expected to grow over time (Olsen, 2012). The most established clubs are airline clubs (the very first was that of American Airlines, which was born in the eighties and currently includes 16 million members) and mobile phone clubs (Nokia, Samsung: online registration enables one to download ringtones, personalize mobile phones, purchase accessories at discounted prices, etc.). Sometimes, a club is created even before the launch of the product, as in the case of the "Yaris Club", which offered to its members information about a car they had not yet purchased. To be effective, the club must include highly distinctive features, in order to enhance the concept of membership, and, second, it must be designed to leverage not only on the users' needs but also on the feelings and emotions that each user feels in the possession or use of a particular product/service.

Clubs have their logical assumption in the concept of membership development, that is, man's natural propensity to gather in groups. This propension, in turn, depends on two concepts derived from social psychology, clanning and the concept of status.

Notes

1. According to the results of a survey conducted in 2003 by Bain & Company, together with Mainspring, in an online clothing store, in order to recover the cost of acquisition, it is necessary that a customer returns four times; this means that the customer must remain loyal to the website for at least 12 months on average. The situation is even worse for online groceries, which are forced to wait 18 months to recover the $80 spent in acquiring a new customer.
2. In retailing, for example, customers become familiar with the product line in the store (Sloot, Fok, & Verhoef, 2006). A customer who repeatedly buys shirts from the same store will eventually notice they also sell footwear. A new customer can enter a car workshop in order to have the wheels balanced or the oil changed, but if he appreciates the service and value received, he will probably switch to more expensive services as tuning the engine and changing the tires. The average revenue per customer in the automotive services triples between the first and fifth year (Reichheld, 1996). In online clothing sales, a loyal customer spends on average 67 % more between the 31st and 36th month than he spent in the first six months, while for grocery stores, that figure rises to 23 %. This difference is due in part to the transaction rate that increases over time, and in part to the magnitude of individual transactions; for example, the fifth online purchase of clothes is on average 40 % larger than the first, the tenth is 80 % larger.
3. As the customer's familiarity with the firm increases, he becomes more efficient: he does not waste time requesting services that cannot be provided, while knowledge of the products makes him less dependent on the information and advice of the firm's staff (Palmatier, Scheer, & Steenkamp, 2007).
4. Another important benefit of long-term relationships is the fact that satisfied customers recommend the company to others. It is necessary to keep in mind that customers acquired by personal recommendation tend to have better features; that is, they tend to be more profitable and stay longer with the company than those conquered by advertising, the ability of sellers, or promotional prices. Customers who approach the company as a result of

recommendations have good reasons for doing so. Customers who are familiar with the company show the pros and cons more accurately than what advertisements or sellers do. Furthermore, since everybody tends to associate with their own kind, the chances are good that customers acquired by recommendations find the services and products offered by the company satisfactory. On average, a customer of a clothing website after the first purchase recommends the website to other three people; after ten purchases, he will recommend it to seven people; and if the website offers hi-tech goods, the number of recommendations reaches 13 after the tenth transaction. In an online environment, this factor becomes even more important both because it is easy to compare the different possibilities and because of the extreme speed at which information spreads.

5. The assertion, often demonstrated in B2C, has been the subject of very limited empirical verification in B2B. One of the objectives of this study, as we shall see in the following chapters, is also the test of this hypothesis.
6. The services required to support the relationship with the customer in the B2B market have been rigorously explored and summarized by Seybold (1999). For a company that wants to put them into practice, it often becomes necessary to develop customized web contents which can be accessed via an extranet, as in the case of services offered to professionals in the industry by Dell in its Premier Pages (Noori & Salimi, 2005).
7. For example, there are only five major companies for the production of trains worldwide (such as ABB Adtranz).
8. In the literature, the argument has been made for the existence of several actors intervening in the decision-making process in B2B: users, influencers, buyers, deciders, and gatekeepers (Webster & Wind, 1996). This complexity is required by the need to ensure financial control and the existence of authorization procedures for the purchase of products that can be very expensive.
9. With the help of website tools, it will be easier for a business customer to evaluate the actual availability of products in stock, orders can be made at any time, repeated orders can be saved and quickly reused, deliveries can be monitored online (and "followed" on the screen thanks to tracking numbers, as it occurs on most of the websites of international carriers), and the order history can be visualized.
10. To facilitate this process, portals such as Yahoo! have been created in order to put buyers in contact with sellers that offer the product corresponding to their needs. Industry.net is a good example of this type of portals, which not only provide information on potential suppliers, but also allow to do research on product specifications, standards, and price lists; the portal now has more than 600,000 registered buyers and thousands of suppliers. Similarly, virtual communities such as Vertical.net also help to support the members of a

specific firm in their purchasing decisions. Many of these intermediaries are currently in the USA, because the US market is very large and tends to be more developed, but some examples are developing also in other markets

11. The guiding principles of the US analyst featured in the book Customer.com (1999) are also available online at the url: www.customer.com.
12. Of course, the shopping script will be induced by the company's customer service through the tools on its website.
13. There is a clear reference to the setup costs in Jones, Mothersbaugh, and Beatty (2002), examined in the phase of literature review.
14. The definition of the term data warehouse has been continuously modified since its inception, which dates back to the early eighties. Some of the definitions mostly used in the literature are the following: (a) a data warehouse is a repository of historical data that is subject oriented, (b) a data warehouse is a set of smaller data marts, (c) a data warehouse is any distinct hardware platform, either a mainframe or a PC, that allows a business user to make decisions.
15. For example, in the case of http://www.Kangaroo.it/welcome.htm?KANGA=hello@Kangaroo.it, the query text is what appears after the question mark (KANGA = hello@Kangaroo.it). In this way, it is possible to link programs in ASP, Java, Javascript, etc. to the log file. It is also possible to see which keywords were used in the search engines.
16. A typical cookie comes in the form RMID#d42d6252399c1080#ilsole24ore.it/#0#3567004032#30124668302416#29362279#*. It is clear that the information contained in cookies is absolutely not understandable by users, and this is one of the reasons why the dominant legal doctrine considers cookies incompatible with user privacy.
17. KDD, and in particular data mining, is not the only way to extract information from a data warehouse, even if it is the most useful for the purpose of studying e-loyalty. Other tools are queries and OLAP (online analytical processing) analysis: a query is a request for information to a database. In this case, a business user makes a specific request to the data warehouse, formulating a strong hypothesis (e.g.: "visualize all customers that purchased the product X in the past four months"). In order to make the operations required to get the desired data more simple and immediate, OLAP analysis tools use a geometric metaphor to represent the universe of data available in the data warehouse (Giudici, 2003). The data is represented in the form of a *n*-dimensional cube (hypercube) which, as a result of an analysis request, is rotated and sectioned in order to extract the desired information. Some of the variables available are located on the sides of the cube (dimensions), while others are the result provided by the analysis (aggregations). This type of approach best summarizes the main feature of OLAP: the possibility to reach the desired information by successive approximations without the

need to formulate precise answers for advanced and complicated requests on the data. There are two types of OLAP analyses, both aimed at multidimensional analysis but differing in the type of approach adopted in the design and creation of the database used for the analyses. The term ROLAP (relational OLAP) indicates the type of OLAP analyses that build the cube using the data contained in a multidimensional database (Evans, 2000). Thus, in conclusion, the terms ROLAP and MOLAP are no more than two ways to indicate the OLAP analyses, different in meaning from the point of view of the creative approach of the database (either relational or multidimensional) but identical from the point of view of the results. Both these types help in performing analyses on the data with the same tools and the same typologies (Kaymak & Setnes, 2000).

18. In MOLAP, the data is cleaned, aggregated in multiple dimensions, and uploaded into a data cube periodically (Gorla, 2003 p. 112).
19. For example, marketing databases contain data on customer purchases, demographics, lifestyle, and financial state, but for the purpose of sales in a department store, only data relating to customer purchases and demographics may be required.
20. The phase in question has a variety of applications. Nowadays, business information systems are focused on structured data and do not allow to properly treat customer information arriving in a textual form through multiple channels (e-mails, phone calls, seller notes, interviews, etc.), neglecting elements that are relevant to the full understanding of customers themselves. A preprocessing phase of documents is text mining, from which structured data is derived to enhance the set of inputs that can be processed with data mining).
21. It is understandable that, in the event of malfunction of the information system, the whole system of customer retention developed can go into crisis: a careless monitoring of a customer's needs, and the possible factors of resistance to change which he can potentially express, can lead to incorrect management of the shopping scripts, increasing the churn rate.
22. An association rule is a valid causal link between attributes of the records in the database. With the search for association rules, as in many data mining techniques, the object of research is known in advance (and this makes the technique particularly interesting from the point of view of the possible commercial applications). In fact, this system seeks on its own what may be interesting for a user, minimizing his intervention.
23. Discovering sequential patterns is a data mining technique used to search for "patterns" within sequences. In many cases, a sequence of events may help to well describe the behavior of systems. Furthermore, by knowing some patterns and their frequency, it is possible to try to predict the evolution of some patterns, and hence of the system.

24. A useful reference on the subject is the contribution by Schafer, Konstan, and Riedl (2003): "E-Commerce Recommendation Applications", available at http://citeseer.nj.nec.com/293817.html.
25. A substantial documentation on information filtering is available at: www.cs.umn.edu/Research/GroupLens.
26. To build effective recommender systems, in addition to collaborative filtering and information filtering, different statistical and data mining techniques can be used at different levels of complexity. The range is from simple algorithms to complicated Bayesian analyses. Information filtering and collaborative filtering are currently by far the most used techniques due to their relative simplicity and effectiveness
27. A typical example of a recommender system that uses collaborative filtering is the B2B section on the Asus.com website, through which computer products (video cards, notebooks, motherboards, barebone PCs, etc.) purchased from other business customers are suggested to clients
28. Web call centers can work through VoIP technology (voice over IP). The term describes the technologies and hardware/software solutions that can transmit the voice signal through data networks based on the IP. To understand VoIP technology, it is necessary to recall the basic concepts of circuit switching and packet switching. The first, used for the voice signal, has these characteristics: (a) the connection is similar to an electrical circuit, open for the duration of the connection itself; (b) a procedure for the call setup is required to establish the signal path and determine the operational parameters; (c) the network reserves to the connection a set number of resources; (d) the band is fixed: if used in part, what advances is not made available to others; (e) the price is based on the duration of the connection and its physical length. In packet switching, the data is "fragmented" into many small "containers" on which the addresses of the sender and the recipient are written; the network nodes sort the packets to their destination, sometimes along different paths. The key points are:

    - the time to cross the network varies from package to package, and reordering mechanisms that introduce delay are required;
    - the call setup and service information are also packaged or attached to the header of the data packets;
    - if a packet is lost, it must be resent: this is also a reason for delay;
    - network resources remain available to all;
    - only the required bandwidth is used;
    - price, based on the volume of traffic, is reduced because the operators are in competition.

    Until now, the two systems were born and raised separately, but the increasing development of data networks has encouraged manufacturers to find increasingly effective methods to "fragment" the voice into IP packets and transmit it as if it were a normal data stream. Thus, VoIP technology was born, and its two main advantages are:

- economy: with an equal amount of data transmitted, a circuit-switched network is very expensive, because it is owned by large operators that operate under a virtual monopoly;
- versatility: it is possible to use private IP backbones extended on one or more countries (intranet) or the World Wide Web.

29. The concept of community, born and theorized in the field of sociology by Tönnies in 1963, is set to become today an interesting business model useful to attract and retain users, thanks to the technology of the Internet and the online world and its progressive virtualization). According to Armstrong and Hagel (Please change 1998 to 1996), the creation of a virtual community logically precedes that of an e-commerce project. If a website is designed as a place where a customer can learn and not only buy, there is a higher chance that he will spend a longer time on the website and later return to visit its pages. To explain this concept, the authors gives some examples, among which is the famous case of Amazon.com. The virtual bookstore, in fact, has not limited itself to online book sales, but acquired some typical features of traditional bookstores, where buyers also go to listen to the advice of experts and exchange ideas and opinions with other readers. From this view, virtual communities play an important role in B2B also. Although in this case, users are professionals in the industry, and hence are better informed on the technical specifications of the products to be purchased, quantities, etc.; thus, virtual forums are often occasions to receive technical advice or suggestions from other professionals, on troubleshooting or guidance on the compatibility of some products, as occurs in the computing and hi-tech products market.
30. Sterne (2000) observed that if a company installs a virtual community on its website, it has positive effects in terms of its brand image, adding value to its products. The American scholar adds that the company should, on the one hand, try to keep intrusions to a minimum, while, on the other hand, it should act as a moderator, fueling discussions and intervening in the case of negative comments.

Bibliography

Alba, J., Lynch, J., Weitz, B., Janiszewski, C., Lutz, R., & Sawyer, A. (1997). Interactive home shopping, consumer, retailer and manufacturer incentives to participate in electronic marketplaces. *Journal of Marketing, 61*(3), 38–53.

Anderberg, M. (1973). *Cluster analysis for applications.* New York: Academic Press.

Armstrong, A. G., & Hagel III, J. (1996). The real value of on-line communities. *Harvard Business Review, 74*(May–June), 134–141.

Balasubramanian, S., Raghunathan, R., & Mahajan, V. (2005). Consumers in a multichannel environment: Product utility, process utility, and channel choice. *Journal of interactive marketing*, 19(2), 12–30.

Baker, P. (1998). *Electronic commerce. Research Report 1998.* London: KPMG Management Consulting.

Balasubramanian, S., & Mahajan, V. (2001). The economic leverage of the virtual community. *International Journal of Electronic Commerce*, 5(3, Spring), 103–138.

Bergen, M., Dutta, S., & Shugan, S. (1996). Branded variants: A retail perspective. *Journal of Marketing Research, 33*, 9–19.

Brougaletta, Y. (1985). What business-to-business advertisers can learn from consumer advertisers. *Journal of Advertising Research, 25*(3), 8–9.

Brüggen, E. C., Foubert, B., & Gremler, D. D. (2011). Extreme makeover: Short- and long-term effects of a remodeled servicescape. *Journal of Marketing, 75*(5), 71–87.

Brown, S. L., & Eisenhardt, K. M. (1997). The art of continuous change: Linking complexity theory and time-paced evolution in relentlessly shifting organizations. *Administrative science quarterly*, 1–34.

Bonfanti, A., Del Giudice, M., & Papa, A. (2015). Italian Craft Firms Between Digital Manufacturing, Open Innovation, and Servitization. *Journal of the Knowledge Economy*, 1–14.

Chung, J. E., Jin, B., & Sternquist, B. (2007). The role of market orientation in channel relationships when channel power is imbalanced. International Review of Retail, *Distribution and Consumer Research, 17*(2), 159–176.

Cummins, S., W. Peltier, J., A. Schibrowsky, J., & Nill, A. (2014). Consumer behavior in the online context. *Journal of Research in Interactive Marketing*, 8(3), 169–202.

Córdoba-Pachón, J.-R., Pilkington, A., & Bernroider, E. (2012). Information systems (IS) as a discipline in the making: Comparing EJIS and MISQ between 1995 and 2008. *European Journal of Information Systems, 21*, 479–495.

Costabile, M. (2001). *Il capitale relazionale: gestione delle relazioni e della customer loyalty.* Milano: McGraw Hill.

Del Giudice, M., Della Peruta, M. R., & Maggioni, V. (2013). The 'Right'knowledge and spin-off processes: an empirical analysis on knowledge transfer. *Journal of the Knowledge Economy*, 4(3), 304–318.

Del Giudice, M. (2004). Turning web surfers into loyal customers: Cognitive lock-in through interface design and website usability. In Y. Gao (Ed.), *Web systems design and online consumer behavior.* New York and Hershey, PA: Idea Publishers.

Edwards, H. K., & Bauer, M. A. (2005, October). A comparison of response time measurement approaches in enterprise information systems. In 2005 IEEE International Conference on Systems, Man and Cybernetics (Vol. 3, pp. 2830–2835). IEEE.

Erasmus, A. C., Boshoff, E., & Rosseau, G. G. (2001). Consumer decision-making models within the discipline of consumer science: A critical approach. *Journal of Family Ecology and Consumer Sciences, 29*, 82–90.

Fill, C. (1999). *Marketing communications—Contexts, contents and strategies* (2nd ed.). Hemel Hempstead, UK: Prentice Hall Europe.

Gilliand, D., & Johnston, W. (1997). Toward a model of business-to-business communications effects. *Industrial Marketing Management, 26*, 15–29.

Giudici, P. (2003). *Applied data mining: Statistical methods for business and industry.* London: Wiley.

Gorla, N. (2003). Features to consider in a data warehousing system. *Communications of the ACM, 46*(11), 111–115.

Hagel, J. (1988). Managing complexity. *The McKinsey Quarterly*, 2, 1–23.

Hamill, J, & Gregory, K. (1997). Internet marketing in the Internationalization of UK SMEs. *Journal of Marketing Management,* Special Edition on Internationalization, J. Hamill (Ed.), 13, 1–3.

Hsu, T., & Chiang, C. (2011). Script comparisons during service encounters in fast-food chains. *Tourism and Hospitality Research, 11*(January), 19–29.

Hutt, M. D., & Speh, T. W. (2012). *Business marketing management: B2B.* Cengage Learning.

Iansiti, M., & West, J. (1997). Technology Integration: Turning Great Research into Great Products, *Harvard Business Review*, may-june 97, 69–79.

Inman, J. J., Winer, R. S., & Ferraro, R. (2009). The interplay among category characteristics, customer characteristics, and customer activities on in-store decision making. *Journal of Marketing, 73*(September), 19–29.

Ivan, B., & Dickson, L. (2008). Consumer economic socialization. In Handbook of consumer finance research (pp. 83–102). Springer New York.

Jacobs, B., & De Klerk, H. M. (2010). Online apparel shopping behaviour of South African professional women: the role of consumers' apparel shopping scripts. *International Journal of Consumer Studies*, 34(3), 255–264.

Jacobs, B., & De Klerk, H. M. (2010). Online apparel shopping behaviour of South African professional women: The role of consumers' apparel shopping scripts. *International Journal of Consumer Studies, 34*, 255–264.

Jacoby, J., & Chestnut, R. W. (1978). *Brand loyalty. Measurement and management.* New York, NY: Wiley.

J. Han, and M. Kamber. Data Mining: Concepts and Techniques, Second Edition. Morgan Kaufmann Publishers, 2007.

Johnson, E. J., Bellman, S., & Lohse, G. L. (2003). Cognitive lock-in and the power law of practice. *Journal of Marketing, 67*, 62–75.

Jones, M. A., Mothersbaugh, D. L., & Beatty, S. E. (2002). Why customers stay: Measuring the underlying dimensions of services switching costs and managing their differential strategic outcomes. *Journal of Business Research, 55*, 441–450.

Kaltcheva, V. D., & Weitz, B. A. (2006). When should a retailer create an exciting store environment? *Journal of Marketing, 70*(January), 107–118.

Kaymak, U., & Setnes, M. (2000). *Extended fuzzy clustering algorithms.* Discussion Paper ERS; ERS-2000-51-LIS, Erasmus Research Institute of Management (ERIM), Erasmus University Rotterdam. Retrieved September 2004, from http://ideas.repec.org/s/dgr/eureri.html

Kotler, P., Armstrong, G., Saunders, J., & Wong, V. (2008). *Principles of marketing.* Prentice Hall Europe.

Kroonenberg, P. M. (2008). *Applied multiway data analysis.* Hoboken, NJ: Wiley.

Le Meunier-FitzHugh, K., & Lane, N. (2009). Collaboration between sales and marketing, market orientation and business performance in business-to-business organizations. *Journal of Strategic Marketing, 17*(3), 291–306.

Lechner, C., & Kreutzer, M. (2010). Coordinating growth initiatives in multi-unit firms. *Long Range Planning, 43*(1), 6–32.

Lee, C., Huang, S., Barnes, F., & Kao, L. (2010). Business performance and customer relationship management: The effect of IT, organizational contingency and business process on Taiwanese manufacturers. *Total Quality Management & Business Excellence, 21*(1), 43–65.

Lee, H. H., & Kim, J. (2008). The effects of shopping orientations on consumers' satisfaction with product search and purchases in a multi-channel environment. *Journal of Fashion Marketing and Management, 12*(2), 193–216.

Liberati, C., & Camillo, F. (2014). Subjective Business Polarization: Sentiment Analysis meets Predictive Modeling. In New Trends in Databases and Information Systems (pp. 329–338). Springer International Publishing.

Lombardo, R., Kroonenberg, P. M., & D'Ambra, L. (2000). Nonsymmetric correspondence analysis: A simple tool in market share distribution. *Journal of the Italian Statistical Society, 9*, 107–126.

Masanell, R. C., & Ricart, J. E. (2010). From strategy to business models and onto tactics. *Long Range Planning, 43*(2), 195–215.

McGrath, R. G. (2010). Business models: A discovery driven approach. *Long Range Planning, 43*(2), 247–261.

Mili, H., Benzarti, I., Meurs, M. J., Obaid, A., Gonzalez-Huerta, J., Haj-Salem, N., & Boubaker, A. (2016). Context Aware Customer Experience Management: A Development Framework Based on Ontologies and Computational Intelligence. In Sentiment Analysis and Ontology Engineering (pp. 273–311). Springer International Publishing.

Moe, W. W., & Yang, S. (2009). Inertial disruption: The impact of a new competitive entrant on online consumer search. *Journal of Marketing, 73*(January), 109–121.

Molina, J. A., Campaña, J. C., & Ortega, R. (2016). Children's interaction with the Internet: Time dedicated to communications and games (No. 68967). University Library of Munich, Germany.

Mougayer, W. (1998). *Opening Digital Markets Battle Plans and strategies for internet commerce.* McGraw-Hill, NY: CommerceNet Press.

Mutula, S. M., & van Brakel, P. (2006). An evaluation of e-readiness assessment tools with respect to information access: Towards an integrated information rich tool. *International Journal of Information Management, 26*(3), 212–223.

Nielsen J., Web usability, Apogeo, Milano, 2000.

Nielsen J., Tahir M., Home page usability, Apogeo, Milano, 2002.

Nielsen, J., & Loranger, H. (2006). *Prioritizing web usability.* Indianapolis: News Riders.

Noori, B., & Salimi, M. H. (2005). A decision-support system for business-to-business marketing. *Journal of Business & Industrial Marketing, 20*(4/5), 226–236.

Olsen, K. A. (2012). How Information Technology is Conquering the World: Workplace, Private Life, and Society. Scarecrow Press.

O'Sullivan, T. (2010). Dangling conversations: Web-forum use by a symphony orchestra's audience members. *Journal of Marketing Management, 26*(7), 656–670.

Oliver, R. L. (1997). *Satisfaction. A behavioral perspective on the consumer.* New York: McGraw Hill.

Palmatier, R. W., Scheer, L. K., & Steenkamp, J. B. E. M. (2007). Customer loyalty to whom? Managing the benefits and risks of salesperson-owned loyalty. *Journal of Marketing Research, 44*(2), 185–199.

Phillips, J. M., & Reynolds, T. J. (2009). A hard look at hard laddering: A comparison of studies examining the hierarchical structure of means-end theory. Qualitative Market Research: An International Journal, 12(1), 83–99.

Poon, S., & Jevons, C. (1997). Internet-enabled international marketing: A small business network perspective. *Journal of Marketing Management, 13*, 29–41.

Prandelli, E., Sahweney, M., & Verona, G. (2008). *Collaborating with customers to innovate: Conceiving and marketing products in the networking age.* London: Edward Elgar Publishing.

Price, L., Arnould, E., & Tierney, P. (1995). Going to extremes: Managing service encounters and assessing provider performance. *Journal of Marketing, 59*(April), 83–97.

Quelch, J., & Klein, L. (1996). The Internet and international marketing. *Sloan Management Review, 37*, 60–75.

Ravasi, D., & Verona, G. (2001). Organising the process of knowledge integration: the benefits of structural ambiguity. *Scandinavian Journal of Management, 17*(1), 41–66.

Reichheld, F. F. (1996). *The loyalty effect.* Boston: Harvard Business School Press.

Rischkowsky, F., & Döring, T. (2008). Consumer policy in a market economy: Consideration from the perspective of the economics of information, the new institutional economics as well as behavioural economics. *Journal of Consumer Policy, 31*, 285–313.

Sawhney, M., & Prandelli, E. (2000). Communities of creation: managing distributed innovation in turbulent markets. *California management review, 42*(4), 24–54.

Schank, R. C., & Abelson, R. P. (2013). Scripts, plans, goals, and understanding: An inquiry into human knowledge structures. Psychology Press, UK.

Schank, R., & Abelson, R. (1977). *Scripts, plans, goals and understanding*. Hillsdale, NJ: Erlbaum.

Schwartz, E. (2000). *Digital Darwinism: Seven breakthrough strategies for surviving in the cutthroat web economy.* New York: Broadway Books.

Selden, L., & MacMillan, I. C. (2006). Manage customer-centric innovation systematically. *Harvard Business Review, 84*(4), 108–116.

Seybold, P. (1999). *Customers.com*. London: Century Business Books, Random House.

Sénécal, S., Fredette, M., Léger, P. M., Courtemanche, F., & Riedl, R. (2015). Consumers' cognitive lock-in on websites: evidence from a neurophysiological study. *Journal of Internet Commerce*, 14(3), 277–293.

Shankar, V., Smith, A. K., & Rangaswamy, A. (2003). Customer satisfaction and loyalty in online and offline environments. *International Journal of Research in Marketing, 20*(2), 153–175.

Shapiro, C., & Varian, H. R. (1999). *Informatiom rules. A strategic guide to the network economy.* Boston: Harvard Business School Press. (Trad. It., *Information rules. Le regole dell'economia dell'informazione*, Milano: Etas, 1999).

Shostak, L. (1977). Breaking free from product marketing. *Journal of Marketing, 41*(April), 32–34.

Simonson, I. (2005). Determinants of customers' responses to customized offers: Conceptual framework and research propositions. *Journal of Marketing, 69*(1), 32–45.

Sloot, L. M., Fok, D., & Verhoef, P. C. (2006). The short- and long-term impact of an assortment reduction on category sales. *Journal of Marketing Research, 43*(November), 536–548.

Smith, J. W. (2006). Coming to concurrence: Improving productivity by reengaging resistant consumers. In J. N. Sheth & R. S. Sisodia (Eds.), *Does marketing need reform?* (pp. 15–25). Armonk, NY: M.E. Sharpe.

Srinivasan, S., & Hanssens, D. M. (2009). Marketing and firm value: Metrics, methods, findings, and future directions. *Journal of Marketing research, 46*(3), 293–312.

Srinivasan, S. S., Anderson, R., & Ponnavolu, K. (2002). Customer loyalty in e-commerce: An exploration of its antecedents and consequences. *Journal of Retailing, 78*(1), 41–50.

Stephen, A. (2004). The emergence of interdependent e-commerce constructs. WSEAS Transactions on Computers, 3(1), 201–208.

Sterne, J. (1999). *World Wide Web marketing* (2nd ed.). New York: John Wiley and Sons.

Sterne, J. (2010). Social media metrics: How to measure and optimize your marketing investment. John Wiley & Sons.

Sterne, J. (2000). *Customer service on internet.* New York: John Wiley and Sons.

Taylor, S. A., Cronin Jr, J. J., & Hansen, R. S. (1991). Schema and script theory in channels research. Marketing Theory and Applications, 2, 15–24.

Tidd, J., & Bessant, J. (2009). *Managing innovation: Integrating technological, market and orgainisational change* (4th ed.). Chichester, England: John Wiley & Sons.

Tsai, S. P. (2005). Integrated marketing as management of holistic consumer experience. *Business Horizons, 48*(5), 431–441.

Turnbull, P. (1999). Business to business marketing: Organisational buying. Behaviour, relationships and networks. In M. Baker (Ed.), *The marketing book* (4th ed.). Oxford: Butterworth-Heinemann.

Tzafrir, S., & Gur, A. (2007). HRM practices and perceived service quality: The role of trust as a mediator. *Research and Practice in Human Resource Management, 15*(2), 1–20.

Van Rekom, J., & Wierenga, B. (2007). On the hierarchical nature of means-end relationships in laddering data. *Journal of Business Research, 60*, 401–410.

Villanueva, J., & Hanssens, D. M. (2007). Customer equity: Measurement, management and research opportunities (No. 1). Now Publishers Inc.

Vrontis, D., & Thrassou, A. (2007). A new conceptual framework for business-consumer relationships. *Marketing Intelligence & Planning, 25*(7), 789–806.

Webster, F., & Wind, Y. (1996). A general model for understanding organizational buying behavior. *Marketing Management, 4*(4), 52–58.

Wells, V., & Foxall, G. (Eds.). (2012) *Handbook of developments in consumer behaviour* (Ed. V. Wells). Durham Business School, Durham University and Gordon Foxall, Cardiff Business School, Cardiff University, UK.

Werner, R. (1985). The environmental psychology of service encounter. In J. Czepiel, M. Solomon, & C. Suprenant (Eds.), *The service encounter. Managing employee/customer interaction in service business* (pp. 101–112). Lexington, MA: Lexington Books.

Wind, J., & Rangaswamy, A. (1999). Customerization. The second revolution in mass customisation. Ebusiness Research Centre Working Paper, EBRC, Penn State Smeal College of Business Administration and School of Information Sciences and Technology, Pennsylvania.

Wicks, R. H. (1992). Schema theory and measurement in mass communication research: Theoretical and methodological issues in news information processing. Annals of the International Communication Association, 15(1), 115–145.

Xu, Y., Goedegebuure, R., & van der Heijden, B. (2006). Customer perception, customer satisfaction, and customer loyalty within the Chinese securities business: Towards a mediation model for predicting customer behavior. *Journal of Relationship Marketing, 5*(4), 79–104.

Yee, R., Yeung, A., & Cheng, T. (2009). An empirical study of employee loyalty, service quality and firm performance in the service industry. *International Journal of Production Economics, 124*(1), 109–120.

Zhang, B., & He, C. (2012). Online customer loyalty improvement: Based on TAM psychological perception and loyal behavior model. *Advances in Information Technology and Management, 1*, 162–165.

Zhao, X., Lynch Jr., J. G., & Chen, Q. (2010). Reconsidering Baron and Kenny: Myths and truths about mediation analysis. *Journal of Consumer Research, 37*(August), 197–206.

CHAPTER 4

Shopping Scripts and Resistance to Change: An Empirical Verification in Business-to-Business Digital Markets

4.1 Theoretical Framework and Research Hypotheses

The literature review carried out in the second chapter has allowed the identification of the major dimensions underlying the developed model. As highlighted, the objective of this study is the empirical verification of customer behavior in a business-to-business (B2B) market. B2B has particular structural connotations: first of all, with regard to the *demographic features of customers* (professionals in the industry compared with end users), their *buying capacity* (in bulk rather than at the retail level), their *bargaining power* (directly linked to a better ability to trade on the types of purchases made in relation to variables such as "time continuity" and "volume of purchases"), and the *determinants of their loyalty* (B2B operators compared with B2B customers tend to be more rational when purchasing. The balance is often given by variables such as price, speed of the purchasing process, product availability, and the elements of customer service. Therefore, as B2B operators are more informed and rational when purchasing, they are potentially more disloyal.) Thus, the literature shows that in a digital economy, and in particular in the B2B sector, the need to induce the creation of a client shopping script is vital for companies that aspire to maximize the spontaneous resistance to change of their customers. The presence of a shopping script provides the individual with a sense of order, organization, and structuring of stimuli from the environment,

M. Del Giudice, M.R. Della Peruta, *The Satisfaction of Change*,
DOI 10.1007/978-3-319-41884-1_4

simplifying the management of cognitive activity (Benjafield, 1992). These benefits inherent in the script would justify a substantial reluctance by individuals to change the buying patterns in use. Moreover, the tendency of consumers in B2B markets to maintain their purchasing patterns, thus speeding up the buying process (which is a critical factor for a company or, more generally, a professional) and not reviewing the assumptions of the established pattern, is precisely the cognitive manifestation of spontaneous resistance to change the acquired patterns (Johnson, 1994).

The literature on cognitive scripts provides a solid theoretical basis for the definition of the concept of script and highlights the benefits associated with its use. But then, recent studies on the interaction between customer and website (Johnson, Bellman, & Lohse, 2003; Lim, 2002; Smith, 2006) confirm that knowledge of a shopping script on the Internet positively affects an individual's ability to complete purchases rapidly, the overall level of control perceived by the user and therefore the overall degree of satisfaction of the individual. In particular, the notion of cognitive control, understood as the predictability of a shopping expedition, a critical factor in B2B where time is a key resource, seems to share one of the advantages of possessing an established shopping script, which can be possibly found, in particular, in stability, order, but above all in the practical possibility of anticipating the process and the outcome of future events (Bateson, 1991).

Moreover, as previously mentioned, the relationship between shopping script and satisfaction has been often maintained in the literature (McCallum & Harrison, 1985; Solomon, Suprenant, Czepiel, & Gutman, 1985), not so much through the theory of perceived cognitive control, but through the theatrical metaphor that knowledge, and respect of a sort of "play script" by every actor involved in the process, ensures a satisfactory final outcome.[1] Thus, as it appeared from the literature review presented in the second chapter, resistance to change shows a desire by the individual (in this case a business customer) to simplify the complexity of decisions and save efforts related to the acquisition and processing of information (which, in our case, has a considerable economic importance for the customer). The still limited presence in the literature of contributions that examine, in digital B2B market, the possession and knowledge of a shopping script and its possible induction of switching costs created by businesses but spontaneously accepted by customers (cognitive lock-in[2]), is the foundation of the empirical analysis and research design developed in the following sections. The precise aim of this study is to provide an empirical contribution to the understanding of the role played by the client script in a market characterized by high churn rates, and to make a methodological contribution to the literature. The research hypotheses can be summarized by the following statements:

H1 : Knowledge of the shopping script has a positive impact on the customer's resistance to change.

H2 : Knowledge of the shopping script has a positive impact on the customer's willingness to pay more.

H3 : Continuity and learning costs, compared with other factors of resistance to change, have a greater impact on the customer's willingness to pay more.

4.2 Choice of the Field of Application of the Research and Methodology Adopted

The statement of the relationship between the creation of a client script, induced by the customer service of an online company, and its development of switching costs with respect to new potential suppliers was subject to empirical verification, by choosing the computer products market and the B2B sector. As reported in the literature, this choice is justified by the complexity and the structural dynamism of such a market. Its structural similarity to a perfectly competitive market as described by Bertrand makes the potential churn rate of its consumers particularly high. The "churn" effect, for the reasons given above, is further enhanced by the choice of empirical verification of the B2B segment. Therefore, it is to be assumed that, for the structural and channel features, and for the types of consumers that operate within it, the market chosen for the empirical verification has all the characteristics to appear as a sector with a high rate of customer disloyalty (the statement is confirmed by several contributions in the literature: Bower, Black, & Turner, 1979; Johnson et al., 2003; Prandelli, Sahweney, & Verona, 2008). Besides, the high level of customer involvement in the buying process and the need to learn a well-defined script in order to maximize the utility function in the purchase seemed to perfectly coincide with the features of the chosen sector.

4.3 Empirical Analysis

The first step of the process of analysis of the client script and its relationship with switching costs led to an exploratory study. The objectives of the latter are summarized in the need to achieve a description of the concept of knowledge of the shopping script and of the main categories of switching costs relative to the market in question. The exploratory phase of the study required the construction of a corpus of data from which information relevant to the examined issue would be extracted in view of later measurement. This phase of scale development was made possible thanks to the in-depth interview technique (Eisenhardt, 1989; Glaser & Strauss, 1967).[3] Thus, in this phase, the survey work consisted in carrying out a series of in-depth interviews with top managers of 20 Italian companies operating in the information technology B2B sector (4 in the role of suppliers and 16 in the role of customers). Upon the establishment of this initial sample, the following were taken into account (Bardin, 1977):

1. the rule of representation, which is to ensure that the corpus is representative of the different perceptions of the respondents[4];
2. the rule of exhaustiveness, which consists in taking into account all the elements that are part of the corpus;
3. the rule of homogeneity of the documents submitted to the verification analysis.[5]

The in-depth interview technique, widely used in marketing research (Evrard, Pras, & Roux, 1993), allows respondents to freely express their opinions within a set of topics defined by the researcher (Bailey, 1994). The basic topics used in this phase of *scale development* were:

- description of the reference website;
- notion of "knowledge" and "lack of knowledge" of the website;
- customer service tools deemed necessary;
- perception of the consequences of knowledge and lack of knowledge of the shopping script;
- perceptions related to changes in the website.

The interviews collected were submitted to a first set of "floating" readings, characterized by the absence of assumptions about the presence of specific elements contained in them, and by the attempt to get a first overview of the subject.

The process, repeated several times, allowed the identification of a number of elements, and then grouped them into categories (the sentences were analyzed in an attempt to bring out the connection and thought patterns that were latent in every interview). Thus, it was possible to achieve the identification of certain categories, corresponding to the initial objectives: the elements related to the knowledge of the shopping script by customers, and the definition of the concept of switching costs in the identified sector. With regard to the first element, in-depth interviews revealed a common element in all respondents: the existence of a shopping script is spontaneously linked to the customers' orientation on the website, and the speed of completion of the shopping expedition. With regard, however, to the second element, the interviews revealed, although transferred in a digital environment, the categories of switching costs already identified in the management literature (Gremler, 1995; Guiltinan, 1989; Heskett, Sasser, & Hart, 1990; Klemperer, 1987a, 1987b; Meng & Elliott, 2009): *lost performance costs*, *uncertainty costs*, *pre-switching search and evaluation costs*, *post-switching behavioral and cognitive costs*, *setup costs*, and *sunk costs*. Thus, this first part of the exploratory factor analysis allowed us to reach some conclusions about the perception of a shopping script by an individual and his attitude with regard to the perception of switching costs associated with the online shopping expedition. Following this stage, the construction of the measuring tool took into account what has emerged so far. Before describing in detail the phase of development of scales and items that characterized the exploratory factor analysis, a methodological premise is required.

At a general level, the literature has shown that shopping scripts are formed by certain fundamental actions, common to all the individuals involved (Abelson, 1981). Moreover, at the individual level, the sequence of actions that characterizes the script is likely to vary from one individual to another (Abelson, 1981). A goal that businesses could pursue, from the perspective of this study, would therefore be to transform a typically "weak" script (the simple operation of buying online) into a "strong" script (a purchase based on rules, routes, times, and well-defined operations in sequence).

The empirical model developed aims at showing precisely, as mentioned, the greater resistance to change of a business customer in the presence of a strong script. This is confirmed even more by the inability of the company to intervene in the process of the customer's purchase: customers make their online purchases in a fully autonomous manner. Therefore, since there is no possibility to intervene at the time of purchase, if an online company wishes to maximize the level of switching costs perceived by its customers, it will have to defer the creation of a strong script to the customer service tools on the website (Sternee, 2000). Moreover, since the customer is fully autonomous at the time of purchase, for the purposes of the empirical analysis, the strong interdependency between knowledge of the shopping script and knowledge of the supplier's website is relevant. The qualitative interviews carried out allowed to highlight that customers evoke their shopping script through the description of their "movements" within the website. This feature refers to the concept of "script trace" suggested by Schank and Abelson (1977). This view is widely supported in the literature, albeit primarily related to nondigital environments. Bowen (1986), in particular, defined "place orientation" as the customer orientation toward the purchasing environment, a concept responsive to the need for an individual's understanding of the environment of the shopping expedition and the path necessary to complete it.[6] Similarly, Titus and Everett (1992) realized that customers "have to fight with the task of orienting themselves within the sales environment" (p. 106).

The contributions of environmental psychology have defined the process described as spatial orientation, "the ability of the individual to determine where he is within an environment and the ability to decide what to do to get to a particular place" (Passini, 1977, quoted by Titus & Everett, 1992, p. 107). From the analysis of the in-depth interviews carried out, it is easy to conceptualize the research design and its reference variables: first, the shopping script is manifested through knowledge of the purchasing environment (the website and the elements of its customer service); second, possession of the shopping script makes a physiological resistance to change spontaneously arise in the customer.

For the purposes of this analysis, a possible consequence of the greater loyalty induced by resistance to change was also tested: the spontaneous willingness of a customer to pay a premium price to preserve the privileges granted by the shopping script developed (this construct is commonly referred to in the management literature as willingness to pay more). The research design, developed in two successive phases, can be summarized as follows:

1. EXPLORATORY FACTOR ANALYSIS → Analysis of factors of resistance to change, conceptualization of shopping script knowledge, and conceptualization of willingness to pay more;

2. CONFIRMATORY MODEL → Hypothesis testing and measurement of the identified constructs.

The in-depth interviews conducted have allowed the generation of an initial pool of scales and items related to the "switching costs" and "shopping script knowledge" constructs[7]; thanks to the support of three professors in the Marketing field at the Grenoble Graduate School of Business, and following the empirical evidence from the literature (Jones, Mothersbaugh, & Beatty, 2002), the items were revised, eliminating those considered nonsignificant for the purposes of this study. The final outcome was an online questionnaire, divided into three sections:

(a) a first section concerning the factors of resistance to change in a digital environment (categorization of switching costs), consisting of 30 items;
(b) a second section concerning the concept of shopping script knowledge, consisting of eight items;
(c) a third section concerning the concept of willingness to pay more, consisting of four items.

Sections (a) and (b) were used in the first phase of this study (development of the exploratory factor analysis). The sub-section (c) was added in the second phase (development of the confirmatory model). Within the process of operationalization of variables, one of the critical choices made concerned the number of points of the measurement scale. In this regard, there is no univocal consensus in the literature on the ideal number of points to be used; the choice often depends on the objectives of the research and the level of accuracy that will hopefully be achieved. In this study, since the primary objective is the accuracy of information, it was decided to adopt a seven-point semantic differential scale (in the literature, these scales are considered easy to understand and use, "universal", and with a satisfactory degree of face validity (Bagozzi, 1994a)).

4.3.1 Exploratory Factor Analysis

The first phase of this study, as mentioned in the previous section, consisted in the development of an exploratory factor analysis, after the collection of data through the questionnaire developed with the support of the in-depth interviews described above.[8] Below are the highlights of the analysis conducted.

4.3.1.1 Sampling Phase

For the constitution of the sample, the customer database of the major B2B distributor of computer products in Italy, Esprinet SpA (www.esprinet.com), was used.[9] From the database, 100 business customers were selected[10] which presented heterogeneous structural features (in order to ensure the representativeness of the chosen sample) but continuity of online purchases (in order to ensure homogeneity in purchase perceptions). Respondents who participated in the study on a voluntary basis and free of charge were asked to respond online, with the aid of a questionnaire ASP resident on the Web and anchored to an SQL Server database. The answering rate (67 %) was significant, demonstrating the interest shown by the top managers of the interviewed firms, to whom the link to the questionnaire and the invitation to participate had been directly addressed. Thus, the first stage returned 67 completed questionnaires from many companies operating in the sale of computer products (hardware, software) at the B2B level. Therefore, exploratory factor analysis was conducted, aimed at determining which latent variables could be significant for the development of the model and for hypotheses testing. Cronbach's alpha analysis revealed overall satisfactory levels of internal consistency of the selected items ($0.83 < \alpha < 0.95$, Table 4.1). The items were later refined and selected to eliminate the latent variables, which did not express enough consistency in relation to the proposed model or did not exhibit a high coefficient of correlation with other items measuring the same construct. The estimate of the internal consistency of all scales selected on completion of the exploratory factor analysis complied with a cutoff loading point > 0.70 (Nunnally & Bernstein, 1994) (Table 4.1).[11]

The analysis of the "shopping script knowledge" construct, for the intrinsic characteristics of the variable, also exhibited a significant value of Cronbach's alpha (0.92). This variable must be analyzed more thoroughly. In the literature, the vast majority of authors (Park, Mothersbaugh, & Feick, 1994, p. 70) make a clear distinction between objective knowledge and subjective knowledge. The first is defined as "the precise information, stored in an individual's long term memory, about a certain category of products". The second is defined, instead, as "the perception by the individual of what he really knows about a certain class of products". In this

Table 4.1 Exploratory factor analysis

Exploratory factor analysis						
Scale/Item	*F1*	*F2*	*F3*	*F4*	*F5*	*F6*
Costs of lost performance (cookie costs) (α = 0.94)[a]						
(1) This online supplier reserves me privileges that I could not find anywhere else.	0.92					
(2) By continuing to buy from the same online supplier, I have benefits I would not have if I changed supplier.	0.91					
(3) There are some benefits that I could not maintain if I changed supplier.	0.94					
(4) I would lose some preferential treatment if I changed supplier.	0.89					
(5) If I changed my current online supplier, I would spend a lot of time and resources to "reproduce" the benefits and privileges inherent in my old buying routine.	0.87					
(6) If I changed my online supplier, it would take me a long time to explain to the new supplier the benefits I had from my previous one.	0.89					
Uncertainty costs (interface tools costs) (α= 0.84)						
(1) I am not sure what level of online customer service I would find if I changed supplier.		0.75				
(2) If I changed my online supplier, the website interface of the new supplier may be more difficult than the current one.		0.81				
(3) If I changed supplier, the customer service of the new supplier's website may be less efficient than the current one.		0.87				
(4) If I changed my online supplier, I could live a less satisfying shopping experience on a new website.		0.85				
(5) My current online supplier gives me interface tools that I could not find anywhere else.		0.88				
Pre-switching search and evaluation cost (web searching costs) (α = 0.86)						
(1) If I changed my online supplier, it would take me a long time to find another one.			0.84			
(2) If I changed my online supplier, it would not take me a long time to find another one.			0.91			

(*continued*)

Table 4.1 (continued)

Exploratory factor analysis						
Scale/Item	*F1*	*F2*	*F3*	*F4*	*F5*	*F6*
(3) It takes a long time to find a new IT online supplier on the Internet.			0.89			
(4) If I stopped buying from my current online supplier, I would have to surf the Internet a lot to find another one.			0.88			
Post-switching behavioral and cognitive costs (interface learning costs) (α = 0.85)						
(1) If I changed my online supplier, I would have to learn the website procedures of the new supplier.				0.79		
(2) I am not familiar with the website of another online supplier as I am with the one of my current supplier.				0.89		
(3) If I changed my online supplier, I would have to learn how the "system" works and every procedure of the new supplier.				0.92		
(4) To change my current supplier would mean to be willing to learn how the website of another supplier works.				0.86		
Setup costs (profile setup costs) (α = 0.95)						
(1) If I changed my online supplier, it would take me a long time to "set up" my profile.					0.95	
(2) If I changed my online supplier, it would not me take a long time to "set up" my profile.					0.92	
(3) If I changed my online supplier, it would take me a long time to explain to the new one "who I am" and "what I need".					0.87	
(4) If I changed my online supplier, it would take me a long time to explain to the new one a lot about my purchases.					0.92	
(5) You need a lot of time and a considerable effort at the beginning of a relationship with a new online supplier.					0.89	
Sunk costs (α = 0.83)						
(1) To build and maintain the relationship with my current supplier many resources, time and energy were required.						0.72

(*continued*)

Table 4.1 (continued)

Exploratory factor analysis

Scale/Item	*F1*	*F2*	*F3*	*F4*	*F5*	*F6*
(2) I have invested a lot in my relationship with my current online supplier.						0.83
(3) All in all, I have invested a lot of resources in my previous purchases with my current online supplier.						0.87
(4) I spent a lot of time and resources learning the purchasing procedure of my current online supplier.						0.86
Eigenvalue	3.95	2.56	10.68	1.92	1.90	1.42
Percent explained variance	14.2	9.4	35.9	6.9	6.8	5.3

Note: In the reported analyses, both the software SPSS version 11.0 and LISREL 8.0 were used.

[a]Following the indications of a previous empirical study conducted together with the Department of Marketing at the Graduate School of Business in Grenoble (Del Giudice, 2004; Poslki & Del Giudice, 2004), in the development of this model, a readaptation of the classic categories of transfer costs to the digital economy is suggested. This revision is simply, in the names, indicating the factors, but it is required by the renewed concept of which they are bearers: cookie costs (costs of lost performance: the new name derives from the use of cookies as factors that induce the shopping scripts "registered" in them), interface tools costs (uncertainty costs: the name arises from the customer's uncertainty regarding the technical interface and design of the new supplier's website), web searching costs (pre-switching search and evaluation costs), interface learning costs (post-switching behavioral and cognitive costs, the new name of which comes from the need to learn the new system), profile setup costs (setup costs), and sunk costs (which retain their original name).

study, following the suggestions of Brucks (1996) and Park et al. (1994), 'both the concept of subjective knowledge and that of objective knowledge have been taken into account, developing three types of questions: an overall measure of subjective knowledge, a measure of subjective knowledge on the various attributes of the website, and a measure of objective knowledge. The first question was intended to measure overall knowledge of the store, asking respondents to rate their knowledge of the reference website (www.esprinet.com) compared with other websites (where they usually stock up).[12] A further question was intended to measure the perceived knowledge of the website's attributes and the presence of an established shopping "path" (simplified, perhaps, by customer service attributes).[13] One last question was focused on the measurement of the objective knowledge of the website by the companies which were interviewed.[14]

4.3.2 *The Confirmatory Model*

The exploratory factor analysis conducted provided valuable support for the definition of the shopping script model.

The second part of this study consists in a more rigorous study of the size of the scales, in order to allow testing of the assumptions made. To develop the confirmatory model and test the hypotheses, the items obtained in the exploratory factor analysis were used (with regard to the switching costs and the knowledge of the script); in addition, also the "willingness to pay more" construct was measured, as a hypothetical outcome of the possession of the script and the resistance to change. This variable, as previously noted, was measured using scales and items adapted from the literature (Zeithaml et al., 1996).[15] The confirmatory model was performed on a larger sample of Esprinet customers: another 180 companies were invited to respond, with similar features to those selected in the sample used for the exploratory factor analysis.[16] The answering rate returned a value of 62 %, confirming the high rate of response and interest in research by the top managers invited to the online questionnaire. Finally, 112 completed questionnaires were available for processing. Thus, the confirmatory model has allowed hypotheses testing (the choice of the test model is perfectly consistent with the recommendations of the management literature on the subject (Gerbing & Anderson, 1988)[17]). The choice of maintaining unaltered the structure of latent variables selected was also justified by the evidence of fit ratios, which showed values that were more than satisfactory.[18] The results obtained showed a good internal strength of each dimension identified in the model; likewise, composite reliability (a measure generated by LISREL, similar to Cronbach's alpha) returned generally high values (Table 4.2). Finally, the variance extracted for each dimension was generally higher than 0.60, indicating a high share of variance between the indicators of each dimension (Fornell & Larcker, 1981).[19]

Hypothesis H1 indicates that knowledge of the shopping script has a generally positive impact on the customer's resistance to change.[20] The confirmatory model developed (Table 4.2) clearly shows this close correlation (the coefficient ϕ varies in the range between 0.21 and 0.67, depending on the referred switching cost). In particular, knowledge of the shopping script is more closely related to the costs of lost performance (ϕ = 0.67) and learning costs (ϕ = 0.54).[21] The test clearly helps to understand the opportunities offered to online businesses operating in

Table 4.2 Confirmatory model

	Phi estimates[a]							
Construct	*1*	*2*	*3*	*4*	*5*	*6*	*7*	*8*
Cookie costs (1)	1.00							
Interface tools costs (2)	0.42	1.00						
	(11.27)[b]							
Web searching costs (3)	0.41	0.44	1.00					
	(10.96)[b]	(11.75)[b]						
Interface learning costs (4)	0.49	0.56	0.27	1.00				
	(12.25)[b]	(13.42)[b]	(5.92)[b]					
Profile setup costs (5)	0.55	0.63	0.39	0.84	1.00			
	(13.15)[b]	(15.75)[b]	(7.92)[b]	(26.63)[b]				
Sunk costs (6)	0.47	0.21	0.34	0.33	0.38	1.00		
	(11.86)[b]	(4.99)[b]	(7.21)[b]	(7.08)[b]	(7.76)[b]			
Knowledge of the shopping script (7)	0.67	0.32	0.25	0.54	0.39	0.21	1.00	
	(16.82)[b]	(6.96)[b]	(5.34)[b]	(12.94)[b]	(7.85)[b]	(4.75)[b]		
Willingness to pay more (8)	0.74	0.49	0.53	0.67	0.55	0.45	0.82	1.00
	(25.89)[b]	(12.44)[b]	(13.27)[b]	(18.61)[b]	(13.32)[b]	(11.90)[b]	(26.22)[b]	
Mean	4.52	4.87	4.25	4.12	4.57	4.69	6.82	6.89
Standard deviation	1.34	1.62	1.83	1.25	1.49	1.94	1.36	1.85
Composite reliability	0.92	0.82	0.89	0.91	0.84	0.85	0.97	0.92
Variance extracted	0.65	0.62	0.68	0.59	0.70	0.68	0.95	0.89

[a]The first number indicates the value acquired by the coefficient ϕ, while the second in brackets is the value of t.

[b]Significant at the level $p > 0.01$.

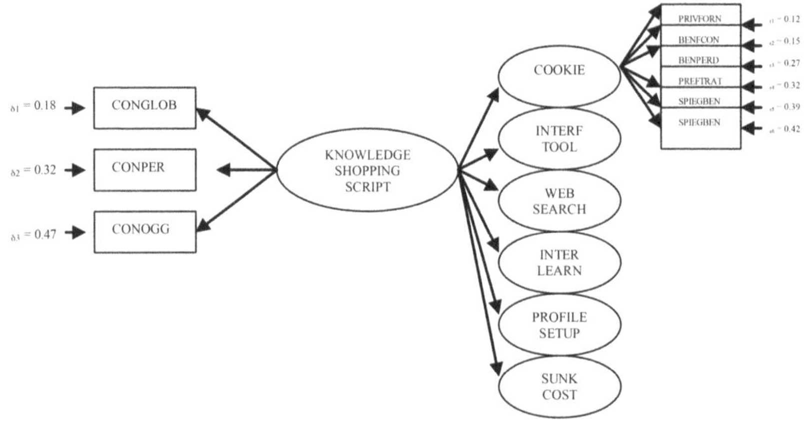

Fig. 4.1 Structural equation modeling for H1: partial graphical representation

the B2B sector by the creation of a client shopping script: the performance obtained through an effective online customer service and the reluctance of customers to abandon established practices to buy from another website, with the risk of increasing purchase time, are a guarantee of loyalty, which cannot be easily eroded.

Similarly, Hypothesis H2 shows an interesting consequence of the construct previously identified. In a B2B market, the cost associated with discomfort and the cognitive effort required to learn how a new website works, along with the perception of satisfaction in using the customer service tools provided by the website which can minimize purchase time, lead professional operators to be also willing to pay a premium price in order to maintain the acquired shopping script and continue to buy from their regular suppliers. The value of the coefficient ϕ in the confirmatory model developed reveals a strong correlation between the customer's willingness to pay the premium price and the established knowledge of a shopping script (ϕ = 0.82). The conclusion has significant importance, first of all from the point of view of the firm, which has the ability to increase its margins, simultaneously with the consolidation of customer loyalty, by leveraging its customer service. And, of course, it provides interesting insights, especially if one bears in mind that such evidence is derived from a market with typically high disloyalty rates.

Finally, Hypothesis H3 seeks to understand the impact of the factors of resistance to change on a plausible customer loyalty, observed from a purely economic perspective: the willingness of a customer to pay more for services featuring the shopping script, which are not retrievable elsewhere in case of switching. The hypothesis aims at investigating in depth what switching costs a business customer perceives to be higher. Resistance to change is manifested, according to the results of the empirical analysis, mainly through two perceived costs: continuity costs (especially those related to the loss of the benefits associated with an established shopping script [costs of lost performance]) and learning costs (especially the costs associated with discomfort and the cognitive effort required to learn how a new website works, in terms of interface design, web architecture, customer service tools, purchasing procedures and information retrieval, etc. [post-switching behavioral and cognitive costs]). In particular, the impact of the costs of lost performance on the customer's willingness to pay more is evidenced by the coefficient ϕ = 0.74; the information transferred by this empirical evidence helps to better understand the importance that learning a shopping script has for a business customer. In case of switching, the business customer would lose all the benefits associated with it and would have to face a too high cost. In fact, the business customer considered in this study buys for reasons strictly related to its business. It may, in fact, be a trade "intermediary" if it is a retailer that resells the products it has purchased, or a producer in a broad sense in the event that it assembles electronic components it has purchased to obtain a finished product to be sold to an end user. From this perspective, it will be particularly oriented to optimize the timing and purchase procedures through the management of a shopping script. The change in the script will have a certain impact on it precisely because it belongs to the B2B sector. In this sector, the time factor and the optimization of purchase procedures are key resources, and have a far greater importance than in the B2C sector, where purchases are generally made not for business, but for personal and emotional purposes of an individual. All this explains better the availability of a business customer to maintain a lively relationship with the previous supplier, even if it means having to pay a premium price for its purchases. For this type of customer, the possibility of maintaining the acquired shopping script is a far-sighted need, as it views the shopping expedition taking into account the past and the future. The past, because it evaluates the benefits associated with the script knowledge (measured by continuity costs), and the future, because it takes into account the need to learn a new system, in the event of switching (measured by learning costs).

Notes

1. In the literature, it is generally argued that knowledge of the activities that a customer has to perform in the buying process improves the evaluation of his satisfaction (Faranda, 1994; Hubbert, 1995; Camelis, Dano, Goudarzi, Hamon & Llosa, 2013). The management literature generally agrees on the importance for a company of teaching a shopping script to its customers, since the latter, facing the changes introduced by the company to improve its productivity, may show some resistance to change, making its implementation difficult (Bateson, 1985b; Lovelock & Young, 1979). A classic example is provided by the amendment introduced years ago by the Italian State Railways in the script "take the train", which consisted in the operation of obliterating tickets in advance. Resistance to change implied for the company a lengthy communication campaign and a long period of initial tolerance toward those who, ignoring the obliteration, resisted to change a script consolidated over time.
2. On the reported limited presence of contributions on the subject and their importance in relation to managerial implications, see Johnson et al. (2003) (as stated in the preface: "Learning is an important factor in electronic environments and efficiency resulting from learning can be modeled with the power law of practice. Most web sites can be characterized by decreasing visit times, [while] those sites with the fastest learning curves show the highest rates of purchasing.")
3. In the definition of scales and items, the indications in the literature of Churchill (1979) and Gerbing and Anderson (1988) have been followed.
4. Compliance with this rule has been assured by selecting companies with structural features (turnover, number of employees, invested capital) different from one another.
5. The corpus of data analyzed for the purpose of this study is "homogeneous", in the sense that it concerns a matter common to all respondents and was obtained through a survey technique identical for all.
6. The literature on the digital economy is still limited on the subject. For a reference to digital contexts, however, see Srinivasan, Anderson, and Ponnavolu (2002).
7. To these constructs "willingness to pay more" was also added, measured by adapting the scales and items present in the literature (Zeithaml, Berry, & Parasuraman, 1996).
8. It should be noted that the questionnaire was pre-tested on 15 randomly selected companies, before being finally used for data collection (by testing it on the exploratory data set). In general, the respondents showed that they were able to answer the questions without any difficulties. However, some clarifications were made to items deemed too general, and the layout quality

was improved. The pre-test results suggested to improve the language of certain statements in the questionnaire and enhance graphics quality. Moreover, the master section was considerably downsized so that the respondents did not perceive the questionnaire as lengthy.

9. Following the methodology reported by Pettigrew (1990), the reference company was chosen on the basis of its visibility in the market, as evidenced by a series of structural indicators accredited in the literature (stock market listing, market share, turnover, number of customers, and number of employees).
10. Bitner (1992) suggested the use of direct observation to understand customer behavior within the environment in which the shopping process takes place (a similar position in the literature, with reference to an offline environment, is maintained by Evrard et al. (1993), p. 128). Since observation is a time-consuming and expensive methodology (Evrard et al., 1993), and difficult to apply in this study, the "method of sample calibration" was preferred, willing to use a methodology that would allow to combine the advantages of observation with those of the questionnaire. The method implied that knowledge of the shopping script was measured on a calibration sample (in this case ten firms), by referring to two websites: Esprinet.com, a website that was "familiar" to users, and Actebis.com, a similar website (for the computer products it markets and its visibility) but "unfamiliar" to them. Knowledge of the shopping script was measured both through perceptual measurements and observed measurements (of course, the calibration sample was required to make a purchase from both websites). Subsequently, the convergent validity between the two measures was calculated (as stated by Heleer and Ray (1972), "a measure may represent a variable in an appropriate manner if it correlates or converges with another measure of this variable, showing that a variable is not only a case of a specific measure", p. 362.) The method uses a quasi-experimentation mode and pursues the objective of verifying the relationship between perceptual measurements and observed, investigating whether perceptions of individuals (obtained through a questionnaire) are reflected in their behavior (detected through direct observation). At the end of this study, after the administration of the questionnaire, the calculation of the correlation between the two latent factors, and perceived and observed knowledge of the script, returned a high coefficient ϕ (= 0.93). The significant convergence between the two constructs was assured by the fact that at a confidence level of 95 % (two standard deviations), the interval for ϕ proved to be equal to $1.07 < \phi < 0.88$. Since the interval contains the value 1, the two factors are not distinct (Bagozzi, 1994b). In other words, the measures of perceptual and observed knowledge converge, suggesting a remarkable consistency between the statements of consumers and their actual behavior.

11. For graphics simplicity, Table 4.1 shows the factor analysis concerning only the factors of resistance to change (appropriately renamed in brackets, in light of the digital economy). With regard to the "knowledge of the script" variable, the value of Cronbach's alpha and the synthesis of the items that characterized the data collection are shown in the text.
12. The question was, *How do you rate your knowledge of this website compared with the others, where you usually stock up?* (the answer involved giving a response on a seven-point Likert scale, from "I hardly know it" to "it is very familiar to me").
13. There were questions on the assessment of *subjective* knowledge of the product catalog, registration procedures, sections with special offers, the order process, the consultation of the shopping cart, the average time of purchase, and simplified shopping paths.
14. To this end, a "true/false/do not know" test was developed on a set of attributes of the website.
15. The measure of Cronbach's alpha for this scale was equally high ($\alpha = 0.87$). Also in this measurement, a seven-point Likert scale was used in order to favor the accuracy of the information detected.
16. The sample constitutes the *confirmatory data set.*
17. Actually, the developed model was tested with an additional confirmatory test that validated its hypotheses, by returning the same results. The need to also use an alternative model is highlighted on several occasions in the literature (Bagozzi, 1994a, 1994b; Gerbing & Anderson, 1988; Hair, Anderson, Tatham, & Black, 1984), and is justified by the need to capture nuances of the impact on the construct variables that a single confirmatory method may omit. In particular, the test was developed through structural equation modeling (SEM), with the support of LISREL 8.0 software. The hypotheses returned the following results. With regard to Hypothesis H1, the SEM returned high values of the coefficient γ. In particular, the positive impact of the "knowledge of the shopping script" variable on the customer's resistance to change showed values such as $0.21 < \gamma < 0.67$, consistent with a measurement error variable in the range of $0.18 < \delta < 0.47$ ($\chi^2 = 39.72$, df [degrees of freedom] = 111, $p < 0.05$; GFI [goodness-of-fit index] = 0.87; AGFI [adjusted goodness-of-fit index] = 0.92).
    For graphical reasons, only a partial graphical representation of the SEM for H1 is presented. For similar reasons of graphical representation, only the endogenous constructs and the relative measurement errors (variable in a range of $0.12 < \varepsilon < 0.42$, as shown in Fig 4.1), connected to the "cookie costs" variable, are shown. The tests of H2 and H3 performed with the SEM, like the confirmatory model developed in the body text of this study, returned the following values: H2 measured a value of $\gamma = 0.82$, with

$0.27 < \delta < 0.52$ ($\chi^2 = 42.54$, df = 111, $p < 0.05$; GFI = 0.91; AGFI = 0.97). H3 recorded $0.74 < \gamma < 0.67$, with $0.19 < \delta < 0.47$ ($\chi^2 = 39.51$, df = 111, $p < 0.05$; GFI = 0.94; AGFI = 0.95). Thus, the structural equations have fully confirmed the relationships highlighted by the confirmatory model based on the ϕ test.

18. Although the χ^2 returned statistically high values ($\chi^2 = 32.87$, df = 111, $p < 0.01$), other fit indices confirmed the full acceptability of the model (Tucker–Lewis index = 0.81, comparative fit index = 0.94; Bollen, 1989). Besides, it is known that the χ^2 is strongly affected by the size of the selected sample.
19. In this study, for the sake of simplicity, the values of the χ^2 difference tests, which were all fully satisfactory, have been omitted.
20. Before commenting on the data, it is advisable to analyze the shape of the distribution of the measured variables. The analysis shows that almost all of the variables in the model present values strongly above average. Moreover, the coefficients of symmetry and kurtosis of the distribution are, respectively, negative (the observations are hence focused on the higher values of the distribution), and positive and high (thus, the observations are highly concentrated). The absence of normality in the distribution is a problem that is frequently found in marketing research. Bagozzi and Baumgartner (1994) and Bagozzi, Baumgartner, and Yi (1992), for example, found in their research that measures of behavioral intention tend to concentrate around the highest values. Similarly, in studies on satisfaction, it often appears that the distribution of observations is not symmetrical, with values that are concentrated at high levels of the measurement scale (Llosa, 1996). It is worth to point out that the choice of a seven-point measurement scale anchored from −3 to +3 was intended precisely to limit the tendency by the respondents to position themselves around the highest values of the scale. However, the precautions taken in the process of data collection are not the only way to rectify non-normality in the distribution. One possible solution to the problem is represented by the transformation of the variables. The Box–Cox method (1964) is a formal method of transformation that, by working residue, consists in finding the kind of transformation that produces residue as close as possible to that of a normal distribution. From calculations made, it appears that the best transformation consists in elevating the variables to the square (although this transformation is not sufficient to normalize the data).
21. A reflection of this validation is given by testing of the following hypotheses, where, among all the switching costs, the highest correlation with the willingness to pay more is recorded precisely by the costs of lost performance ($\phi = 0.74$) and the learning costs ($\phi = 0.67$).

Bibliography

Abelson, R. (1981). Psychological status of the script concept. *American Psychologist, 36*(7), 715–729.

Bagozzi, R. (Ed.) (1994a). *Principles of marketing research.* Oxford, UK: Blackwell Publishers.

Bagozzi, R. (Ed.) (1994b). *Advanced methods of marketing research.* Oxford, UK: Blackwell Publishers.

Bagozzi, R., & Baumgartner, H. (1994). *The evaluation of structural equations models and hypothesis testing.* In R. Bagozzi (Ed.). (1994a), *Principles of marketing research.* Oxford, UK: Blackwell Publishers.

Bagozzi, R., Baumgartner, H., & Yi, Y. (1992). Appraisal processes in the enactment of intentions to use coupons. *Psychology and Marketing, 9*, 469–486.

Bailey, K. (1994). *Methods of social sciences.* New York: The Free Press.

Bardin, L. (1977). *L'analyse du contenu.* Paris: Presses Universitaires de France.

Bateson, J. (1985, Fall). Self-service consumer. An exploratory study. *Journal of Retailing*, 61(3), 49–76.

Bateson, J. (1991). Understanding service consumer behavior. In C. Congram & M. Friedman (Eds.), *The AMA handbook of marketing for the service industries* (pp. 135–150). New York: AMA.

Benjafield, J. (1992). *Cognition.* Englewood Cliffs, NJ: Prentice Hall. (Trad. It., *Psicologia dei processi cognitivi*, Bologna: Il Mulino, 1995).

Bitner, M. J. (1992). Servicescapes: The impact of physical surroundings on customers and employees. *Journal of Marketing, 56*(April), 57–71.

Bollen, K. A. (1989). *Structural equations with latent variables.* New York: Wiley.

Bowen, D. (1986). Managing customers as human resources in service organizations. *Human Resource Management, 25*(Fall), 371–383.

Bower, G., Black, J., & Turner, T. (1979). Script memory for text. *Cognitive Psychology, 11*, 177–220.

Box, G. E. P., & Cox, D. R. (1964). An analysis of transformations. *Journal of the Royal Statistical Society, Series B (Methodological), 26*, 211–252.

Brucks, M. (1996). A typology of consumer knowledge contents. In R. Lutz (Ed.), *Advances in consumer research, vol. 13, Proceedings of the 16th Annual Conference* (pp. 58–63). Provo, UT: Association for Consumer Research.

Churchill Jr., G. A. (1979, February). A paradigm for developing better measures of marketing constructs. *Journal of Marketing Research, 16*, 64–73.

Camelis, C., Dano, F., Goudarzi, K., Hamon, V., & Llosa, S. (2013). The roles of co-clients and their influence on overall satisfaction during the service experience. Recherche et Applications en Marketing (English Edition), 28(1), 42-64.

Del Giudice, M. (2004). Turning web surfers into loyal customers: Cognitive lock-in through interface design and website usability. In Y. Gao (Ed.), *Web systems design and online consumer behavior*. New York and Hershey, PA: Idea Publishers.

Eisenhardt, K. M. (1989). Building theories from case study research. *Academy of Management Review, 14*(4), 532–550

Evrard, Y., Pras, B., & Roux, E. (1993). *Market, etudes et recherches en marketing*. Ed. Nathan. Paris.

Faranda, W. (1994). *Customer participation in service production: An empirical assessment of the influence of realistic service previews*. Unpublished doctoral dissertation, Arizona State University.

Fornell, C., & Larcker, D. F. (1981). Evaluating structural equation models with unobservable variables and measurement error. *Journal of Marketing Research, 18*, 39–50.

Gerbing, D. W., & Anderson, J. C. (1988). An updated paradigm for scale development incorporating unidimensionality and its assessment. *Journal of Marketing Research, 25*(May), 186–192.

Glaser, B., & Strauss, A. (1967). *The discovery of grounded theory*. Chicago: Aldine.

Gremler, D. (1995). *The effect of satisfaction, switching costs and interpersonal bonds on service loyalty*. Unpublished doctoral dissertation, Arizona State University.

Guiltinan, J. (1989). A classification of switching costs with implications for relationship marketing. In T. Childers, R. Bagozzi, J. Peter, et al. (Eds.), *AMA winter educators' conference: Marketing theory and practice* (pp. 216–220). Chicago: AMA.

Hair, J., Anderson, R., Tatham, R., & Black, W. (1984). *Multivariate data analysis*. New York: Maxwell Macmillan International Editions.

Heleer, R., & Ray, M. (1972). Measure validation in marketing. *Journal of Marketing Research, 9*(November), 361–370.

Heskett, J., Sasser, W., & Hart, C. (1990). *Service breakthroughs: Changing the rules of the game*. New York: The Free Press.

Hubbert, A. (1995). Customer co-creation of service outcomes: Effect of locus of causality attributions. Unpublished doctoral dissertation, Arizona State University.

Johnson, B. T. (1994). Effects of outcome-relevant involvement and prior information on persuasion. *Journal of Experimental Social Psychology, 30*(6), 556–579.

Johnson, E. J., Bellman, S., & Lohse, G. L. (2003). Cognitive lock-in and the power law of practice. *Journal of Marketing, 67*, 62–75.

Jones, M. A., Mothersbaugh, D. L., & Beatty, S. E. (2002). Why customers stay: Measuring the underlying dimensions of services switching costs and managing their differential strategic outcomes. *Journal of Business Research, 55*, 441–450.

Klemperer, P. (1987a). Markets with consumer switching costs. *Quarterly Journal of Economics, 102*, 375–394.

Klemperer, P. (1987b). The competitiveness of markets with switching costs. *RAND Journal of Economics, 18*(1), 138–150.

Lim, S. (2002). The self-confrontation interview: Towards an enhanced understanding of human factors in web-based interaction for improved website usability. *Journal of Electronic Commerce Research, 3*(3), 162–173.

Llosa, S. (1996). Contribution à l'étude de la satisfaction dans les services. Thèse pur le Doctorat Nouveau Régime.

Lovelock, C., & Young, R. (1979). Look to consumer to increase productivity. *Harvard Business Review, 57*(May–June), 168–179.

McCallum, J., & Harrison, W. (1985). Interdependence in the service encounter. In J. Czepiel, M. Solomon, & C. Suprenant (Eds.), *The service encounter. Managing employee/customer interaction in service business* (pp. 35–48). Lexington, MA: Lexington Books.

Meng, J., & Elliott, K. M. (2009). Investigating structural relationships between service quality, switching costs, and customer satisfaction. *The Journal of Applied Business and Economics, 9*(2), 54–67.

Nunnally, J. C., & Bernstein, I. H. (1994). *Psychometric theory* (3rd ed.). New York, NJ: McGraw-Hill.

Park, C., Mothersbaugh, D., & Feick, L. (1994). Consumer knowledge assessment. *Journal of Consumer Research, 21*(June), 71–82.

Passini, R. (1977). Wayfinding: A study of spatial problem solving with implications for physical design. Unpublished dissertation, Pennsylvania State University.

Pettigrew, A. (1990). Longitudinal field research on change: Theory and practise. *Organization Science, 3*, 267–292.

Prandelli, E., Sahweney, M., & Verona, G. (2008). *Collaborating with customers to innovate: Conceiving and marketing products in the networking age*. London: Edward Elgar Publishing.

Schank, R., & Abelson, R. (1977). *Scripts, plans, goals and understanding.* Hillsdale, NJ: Erlbaum.

Smith, J. W. (2006). Coming to concurrence: Improving productivity by reengaging resistant consumers. In J. N. Sheth & R. S. Sisodia (Eds.), *Does marketing need reform?* (pp. 15–25). Armonk, NY: M.E. Sharpe.

Solomon, M., Suprenant, C., Czepiel, J., & Gutman, E. (1985). A role theory perspective on dyadic interactions: The service encounter. *Journal of Marketing, 49*(Winter), 95–111.

Srinivasan, S. S., Anderson, R., & Ponnavolu, K. (2002). Customer loyalty in e-commerce: An exploration of its antecedents and consequences. *Journal of Retailing, 78*(1), 41–50.

Sternee, J. (2000). *Customer service on internet.* New York: John Wiley and Sons.

Titus, P., & Everett, P. (1992). The consumer retail search process: A conceptual model and research agenda. *Journal of the Academy of Marketing Science, 23*(2), 106–119.

Zeithaml, V. A., Berry, L. L., & Parasuraman, A. (1996). The behavioral consequences of service quality. *Journal of Marketing, 60*(April), 31–46.

CHAPTER 5

Managerial Implications of the Model and Final Insights

5.1 Final Insights

The issue addressed in this study is part of the debate on customer retention tools available to online businesses operating in business-to-business (B2B) markets and on the ability of the latter to induce in customers the creation of established purchase paths (shopping scripts) capable of increasing their loyalty through a greater and voluntary resistance to change. The limited presence of empirical analyses in the B2B sector is the strong point and the main innovation of this study. Following the analysis of the different contributions that make up the theoretical framework of the research, it was proposed to investigate the relationship between knowledge of the shopping script of online goods or services by customers and the perceived cost of switching to a potential new supplier.

The final outcome of the literature review carried out in the second chapter, and the analysis of the tools available to online businesses to structure an effective customer service, enabled the development of hypotheses, marking the transition from purely theoretical work to research methodology. Since it focuses on a digital market, the research led to greater difficulties as it was referred to an online context. Of course, the choice of the computer products industry as a reference laid the foundation for the analysis of a context characterized by strong purchase criticalities: first, because it is characterized by a structure very similar to that of competitive markets as described by Bertrand, and second, because it expresses high rates of customer disloyalty, also for the influence of the "channel" effect.

M. Del Giudice, M.R. Della Peruta, *The Satisfaction of Change*,
DOI 10.1007/978-3-319-41884-1_5

The results obtained allow to draw some conclusions which are the scientific contribution of this work. A first observation is certainly the concept of cognitive script. This has proved to be perfectly consistent with the nature of the concept of online purchasing and, accordingly, has been confirmed as a theory useful to describe and represent a customer's online behavior and its possible consequences on the work and the outcomes pursued by the supplier. Thus, a first outcome may be found in the real opportunity of using the concept of script beyond its purely descriptive and metaphorical meaning (the classic "theatrical script" mentioned in several parts of the literature), combining the results achieved in previous decades by cognitive psychology with the cognitive objectives typical of the study of the behavior of customers and B2B online businesses (Shankar, Smith, & Rangaswamy, 2003; Zhang & He, 2012).

The developed research has confirmed, although tangentially, that measures of subjective and objective knowledge of some aspects of the buying process can be good indicators of knowledge (and use) of a script. It is important to reach such a conclusion because it provides a contribution to the problem of differences between perceptual measures and observation measures, which is an important issue in marketing research (Dubois & Qaghebeur, 1997).[1] Of course, the major result that emerges from this study is the validation of the model based on the core hypotheses of the research: in a B2B online market, the knowledge and possession of a shopping script by a business customer have a direct impact on switching costs. In particular, the empirical analysis conducted showed that among the switching costs, continuity and learning costs are more related to the knowledge of a shopping script.

This evidence has a double meaning. On the one hand, it leads one to think over the "technical" nature of a shopping script in a digital economy: the possession of a script is closely linked to the possession of knowledge affecting the customer's ability to take full advantage of a website that is able to offer an efficient and comprehensive customer service (through a variety of tools, templates, elements of interface design and web architecture, preferential pathways, etc.). Moreover, it confirms what was recently reported in the literature (Johnson, Bellman, & Lohse, 2003): in the B2B sector (but probably this sector above all, given the nature of the actors), the websites whose users show the fastest learning curves are also those that have the highest sales and repurchase rates. Basically, a loyal customer is an "expert" and "fast" customer, that is, he is able to rapidly learn "how the system works" and how to conclude his shopping expedition quickly.

As such, it is a business customer that maximizes its revenues by compressing shopping time (in the B2B sector, time-based competition is an absolute requirement) and optimizing its purchasing operations.

This study represents one of the first empirical contributions on the subject, especially because it attempts to provide empirical support to a statement often cited in the literature (the correlation between knowledge of the script and resistance to change). And it is indeed a confirmation of the reflections and the outcomes achieved in other disciplines (such as services marketing) in relation to the difficulties and the reluctance of individuals to change their cognitive schemas. The knowledge of a script essentially allows an individual to deal with the information more easily and rapidly, and subsequently, to promptly activate behavior appropriate to the type of schema (Iederan, Curseu, Vermeulen, & Geurts, 2011). The bounded rationality of a business customer, that faced with new situations will tend to immediately utilize available schemas and use as a basic rule of its decision-making process the repetition of a situation it is familiar with, is immediately translated into the perception of a cost toward the change of its *modus operandi* (resident in the shopping script).

An immediate reflection with regard to the data obtained from the empirical analysis certainly lies also in the broader concept of perceived risk. A customer does not exclusively perceive a cognitive cost directly linked to the change of a now acquired and consolidated behavior (and hence the loss of benefits provided by the previous website or the need to learn a new one), but also the risk of not being able to find, from another supplier, the same conditions that gave birth to the script. Of course, by its very nature, the process of online purchasing, on the one hand, reassures customers by presenting low research costs and limited psychological costs (sunk costs), while on the other, it amplifies the concept of risk and uncertainty. The intangibility and the difficulty in evaluating in advance the website's features, and the uncertainty linked to the practical usability of a new supplier's website, can make customers particularly sensitive to the risks which can be associated with the switch. In this view, longevity of the relationship and the shopping script would provide the customer with real benefits, already sufficiently investigated by the literature: the perception of fairness in services rendered and advance knowledge of the features of the shopping expedition.[2] It is interesting to note that certain switching costs show increased correlation with the knowledge of the shopping script: this evidence is mainly due to the focus of this research on a digital market, which is business intensive and characterized by structural change and dynamism. A logical consequence is the empirical evidence confirming that management can focus on the elements of customer service that maximize continuity and learning costs for customers to ensure that their companies increase their profitability, consistently, with a churn rate under control.

5.2 Managerial Implications of the Research

An immediate consideration that emerges from the theoretical analysis arising from this study concerns the use of the concept of script as a tool for understanding the way a customer (in our case a company or a professional in the computer industry) lives his shopping expedition. The observation of the customer when using his shopping script is a way to obtain precise information on the way the customer lives the script itself. Of course, in this study, focusing on the B2B sector implies the creation of a behavioral script that is substantially different, for example, from the business-to-customer (B2C) sector. This is because, as it has been widely demonstrated, the expressed needs vary according to the channel level, inducing behavior based on different scripts. In this view, the evocation of the script by the customer can be a way for the seller to learn more about how the customer perceives the sequence in the delivery process of the service. A managerial implication of fundamental importance lies precisely in the perception of the shopping script by the customer. Resistance to change was typically justified by the classical economists through the "lock-in cycle" (Shapiro & Varian, 1999). From this view, the lock-in has been discussed in the literature as a subtle strategy that would tend to "entrap" the customer (Shapiro & Varian, 1999), not so much because, to say it in Hirschman's words, he "wants" to be loyal, but because he "has to" be loyal (Hirschman, 1970). Thus, the strategy of loyalty in question would assume, from this point of view, a strongly negative connotation: loyalty is induced by the lack of real alternatives or an excessive reconversion cost for the customer. Therefore, he would not be cognitively loyal because he is satisfied, but he would repeat his purchases for a kind of inertial behavior.

The logic of this study reverses the traditional way of considering the lock-in, providing B2B companies engaged in the digital environment with interesting managerial perspectives of customer loyalization. A second consideration concerns, instead, the participation of business customers in the definition of the shopping script. Although the script reflects the representation that an individual builds of his online shopping experience, this does not prevent the supplier, as it emerged in the third chapter, from identifying, by trying to assume the customer's point of view, the actions the latter is required to perform within the script, to instruct him through informative material or contact staff (as, for example, in the case of web call centers). Since both the marketing literature and the present study have shown that the perception of a learning cost related to the functioning of a new website and the risk of a final outcome lower than the current are inherent in the knowledge and possession of the shopping script, it appears to be crucial, from a managerial point of view, to help customers build the shopping script in order to create in them a level of psychological comfort and ease of use of the schema that makes the idea of changing behavior not very interesting or attractive. Besides, the creation of the shopping script, as seen in the third chapter, can count on a variety of tools and technologies (not least also newsletters or informative e-mails). A further consideration, however, concerns changes to an existing script. This study focused on the analysis of switching costs in relation to a new supplier. However, the outcomes obtained are an element of reflection for those businesses that, as a result of a change of technology, implementation of new customer service tools, or, more simply, as a result of their efforts to improve the quality of their website, modify the script definition process. For such businesses, the resistance by customers to learn a new shopping script could paradoxically lead to a technological regression to less advanced forms of script. An example of this is the hotel chain Hilton, which, some years ago, had installed information systems that allowed customers to check-out while comfortably seated in their rooms. Through the use of a television and a remote control, customers could view the amount of their bill and pay by credit card. But after some time, the deputy marketing director of the chain had to admit that the system had been suppressed, simply because "customers did not like it". Such a form of payment, even if seemingly more convenient, forced customers to modify a script they already knew and invest in learning an alternative form of payment, which was, at that time, less pleasant and, to some extent, perceived as potentially risky.[3]

A further managerial implication is also suggested by the analysis of the literature review discussed in the second chapter. Some of the literature analyzed showed that a correct learning of the script by a business customer is a necessary, though not sufficient, condition for the perception of the quality of customer service provided by the supplier through its website. The logic underlying this statement lies in the very nature of a shopping script: it includes behavior, actions, and expected contexts of a customary event. The combination of these elements represents the set of expectations related to which customers will compare the level of service actually received. As a result, the supplier will have to make sure that the gap between the expectations contained in the shopping script and the performance perceived in the shopping experience is low or null. While, on the one hand, the customer learns the script through the shopping expedition, building expectations through the shopping experience, on the other hand, the role of accurate information is also important. In other words, the company can teach the script to its customers during the first shopping experience or even before the experience itself (as in the case of corporate clubs). Therefore, at this point, a further aspect has to be considered: the appreciation of the script by the customer.

The activity of evocation and activation of the script is essentially cognitive; nevertheless, the different elements that make up the script can be evaluated by the customer. Customer satisfaction surveys often evaluate the final outcome of the shopping expedition, without considering possible alternatives deviant from the basic shopping script, which nevertheless ensure a positive result. The reference is to a procedural aspect of the shopping experience: the sequence of actions that make up the shopping script. Some questions may inspire debate, suggesting paths of development for managers and entrepreneurs: which sequence is more suitable? Is the current sequence logical for the customer, or is it exclusively for business? Considerations like these can certainly help the management to also take into account the customer's point of view within service operations. Ultimately, it is worth to think over another consideration regarding changes to existing scripts.

The dynamic nature of digital markets and the eclecticism of customers imply a considerable attention of the staff responsible for the management of online customer service: the needs of business customers may change over time and reflect the need for a different script. The management should therefore be prepared to analyze the consequences of this change on the business system, through the management of an effective information system. Thus, if, on the one hand, it will play an active role in the management of the scripts (transfer and teaching of the cognitive schema to the customer), on the other hand, it will have to be ready to intervene on the validity and efficiency of its components so it does not have to manage subsequent competitive delays or undergo switching attempts.

5.3 Limits of the Present Research

The developed research shows, of course, some limits which must be pointed out. First, with regard to the modeling of the highlighted relationships, in order to reduce the complexity and potential numerousness of relationships to be analyzed, a direct correlation between the level of knowledge of a shopping script in a digital economy and the factors of resistance to change by a customer was sustained. It is reasonable to presume the existence of latent variables as mediators of such a relationship, such as "perceived control" and the "concept of habit" (which may more thoroughly explain the examined phenomenon). Another limit of this study is the operationalization of the concept of shopping script. The latter, although perfectly consistent with the type of market examined in this study, is limited to the actions taken by a website's user in a unique and unidirectional way. Future perspectives are instead toward forms of two-way interaction between the website and the customer (as the possibility of online chats directed to pre- and after-sales support). These elements of interaction, for ease of study, were not included in our operationalization. Finally, the major limit, like that of most marketing research, however necessarily required, is inherent in the generalizability of the findings: this study was conducted on a specific market (that of computer products) at a precise channel level (B2B). The choice of this combination, made with the aim of testing a market with high rates of structural disloyalty, is not however the only feasible one.

5.4 Ideas for Future Research

A first opportunity for future research may be the replica of the proposed model to other markets (online, but also offline) or channel levels (B2C, C2C, B2A, etc.). Of course, any changes induced in the model require the researcher to investigate the features of the specific nature of the script in question, which is a necessary and sufficient condition so that the customer perceives a reluctance to change supplier. Another consideration regards the application potential of the concept of script itself. On the one hand, as noted in the previous section, it would be interesting to analyze in greater detail the correlation between knowledge of the shopping script and customer resistance to change. The possible emergence of mediating variables may be a moment of further consideration for research. Still, given the lack of empirical contributions in the literature on the effects on a company of the knowledge of a client's shopping script, the construct could be analyzed more in depth. This study, in part, is tangent to a similar aspect, because it considers, from the perspective of an online company, the design of a website oriented to the creation of a shopping script for a customer that makes him satisfied and reluctant to change.

It would thus be interesting to verify more in depth the learning effects of the script on the overall level of efficiency of the system and its overall productivity. Finally, it may be interesting to observe the effects of "voluntary deviations" of the script on the level of customer satisfaction.

If, on the one hand, the exhaustiveness of the paradigm of confirmation/disconfirmation of expectations could be questioned, on the other hand, the voluntary deviation could be a useful opportunity for a company to reflect on the advisability of intervening in the script acquired by the customer, inducing voluntary changes aimed at surprising and satisfying him.

Notes

1. Dubois and Qaghebeur wrote, in fact, that "knowing if consumers actually do what they say is of outstanding methodological importance" (1997, p. 894).
2. The perception of fairness is an important relational construct, considered both in the studies on customer satisfaction and those on relationship marketing. In particular, studies on social psychology (Austin, McGinn, & Susmilch, 1980; Homans, 1961) showed that the concept of fairness is attributable to proportionality, as perceived by the customer, between the outputs (benefits) and the inputs (sacrifice costs) of an exchange, and the outputs and inputs that are generated by the same exchange for a third party. The application of this definition of equity to research on customer satisfaction (Guenzi, Georges, & Pardo, 2009; Oliver & Swan, 1989a, 1989b; Swan & Mercer, 1981) later showed that this perception may affect satisfaction levels in a negative way—or positive in the case of a proportion between output and input favorable to customers (Andersen & Kumar, 2006). In this regard, it has been suggested that the low fairness perceived in strictly dyadic terms or in terms of discrimination of sales conditions compared with other customers ends up generating in customers a perception of opportunism by the counterparty (the supplier), which depresses the overall level of satisfaction. The negative influence on satisfaction, which usually occurs after the perception of unfairness in the terms of trade, can produce an increase in the level of expectations (which in the case of transaction and consumption that have already taken place will consist in retrieved expectations) or reduce the performance perceived (Brown, Cobb, & Lusch, 2006).

In both cases, the origin should be attributed to unfairness perceived in the terms of trade. Therefore, in this sense, the perception of unfairness in a trade would act as a particular form of cognitive dissonance (Huppertz, Arenson, & Evans, 1978), modifying the degree of satisfaction either directly or by acting on the perception of its determinants. In this sense, a moderate fairness of the terms of trade does not cause dissatisfaction if supported by the perception of reciprocity, so sacrifices in the short term are offset by recoveries of fairness in the medium-to-long term (serial fairness) (Ganesan, 1994). Basically, the options of self-interest maximization are prevented from being exercised in the short term, and an exchange perceived as unfair is, however, considered satisfactory if there is a belief that the future trade will re-establish the overall "balance" of the relationship.

3. A similar incident occurred years ago in the information technology B2B industry when the multinational Computer 2000 (today Techdata SpA) changed the procedure of orders in the name of a technological overhaul: a simple software for ordering online was replaced by a real database locally resident, but upgradeable via the Internet, which, while still allowing a higher number of check & order operations than the previous version, caused a decrease in purchases since many customers were reluctant to learn the new script.

Bibliography

Andersen, P. H., & Kumar, R. (2006). Emotions, trust and relationship development in business relationships: A conceptual model for buyer-seller dyads. *Industrial Marketing Management, 35*(4), 522–535.

Austin, W., McGinn, N. C., & Susmilch, C. (1980). Internal standards revisited: Effects of social comparisons and expectancies on judgments of fairness and satisfaction. *Journal of Experimental Social Psychology, 16*, 426–441.

Brown, J. R., Cobb, A. T., & Lusch, R. F. (2006). The role played by interorganizational contracts and justice in marketing channel relationship. *Journal of Business Research, 59*(2), 166–175.

Dubois, B., & Qaghebeur, A. (1997). Les consommateurs, font-ils ce qu'il disent? In *Actes du 13ème Congrès de l'Association Française du Marketing* (pp. 891–905). Toulouse, May 29–30.

Ganesan, S. (1994). Determinants of long-term orientation in buyer-seller relationship. *Journal of Marketing, 58*(April), 1–19.

Guenzi, P., Georges, L., & Pardo, C. (2009). The impact of strategic account managers' behaviors on relational outcomes: An empirical study. *Industrial Marketing Management, 38*(3), 300–311.

Hirschman, A. O. (1970). *Exit, voice and loyalty. Responses to declines in firms, organizations and states.* Cambridge, MA: Harvard University Press.

Homans, G. C. (1961). *Social behavior: Its elementary forms.* New York, NY: Brace & World, Hartcourt.

Huppertz, J. W., Arenson, S. J., & Evans, R. H. (1978). An application of equity theory to buyer-seller exchange situations. *Journal of Marketing Research, 15*(May), 250–260.

Iederan, O. C., Curseu, P. L., Vermeulen, P. A. M., & Geurts, J. L. A. (2011). Cognitive representations of institutional change: Similarities and dissimilarities in the cognitive schema of entrepreneurs. *Journal of Organizational Change Management, 24*(1), 9–28.

Johnson, E. J., Bellman, S., & Lohse, G. L. (2003). Cognitive lock-in and the power law of practice. *Journal of Marketing, 67*, 62–75.

Oliver, R. L., & Swan, J. E. (1989a). Consumer perceptions of interpersonal equity and satisfaction in transactions: A field survey approach. *Journal of Marketing, 53*(April), 21–35.

Oliver, R. L., & Swan, J. E. (1989b). Equity and disconfirmation perceptions as influences on merchant and product satisfaction. *Journal of Consumer Research, 16*(December), 372–383.

Shankar, V., Smith, A. K., & Rangaswamy, A. (2003). Customer satisfaction and loyalty in online and offline environments. *International Journal of Research in Marketing, 20*(2), 153–175.

Shapiro, C., & Varian, H. R. (1999). *Informatiom rules. A strategic guide to the network economy.* Boston: Harvard Business School Press. (Trad. It., *Information rules. Le regole dell'economia dell'informazione*, Milano: Etas, 1999).

Swan, J. E., & Mercer, A. A. (1981). Consumer satisfaction as a function of equity and disconfirmation. In R. L. Day & H. K. Hunt (Eds.), *Refining concepts and measures of customer satisfaction and complaining behavior* (pp. 7–12). Bloomington, IN: Indiana University.

Zhang, B., & He, C. (2012). Online customer loyalty improvement: Based on TAM psychological perception and loyal behavior model. *Advances in Information Technology and Management, 1*, 162–165.

Bibliography

Adam, N. R., Dogramaci, O., Gangopadhyay, A., & Yesha, Y. (1999). Electronic commerce: Technical, business, and legal issues. Englewood Cliffs, NJ: Prentice Hall.

Agarwal, R., & Karahanna, E. (2000). Time flies when you're having fun: Cognitive absorption and beliefs about information technology usage. MIS Quarterly, 24(4), 665–694.

Agrawal, V., Arjona, L. D., & Lemmens, R. (2001). E-performance: The path to rational exuberance. The McKinsey Quarterly, 1, 31–43.

Alba, J., & Hasher, L. (1983). Is memory schematic? Psychological Bullettin, 93(2), 203–231.

Allen, C., Kania, D., & Yaeckel, B. (1998). Internet world guide to one-to-one web marketing. New York: Wiley and Sons.

Amit, R., & Zott, C. (2001). Value creation in e-business. *Strategic Management Journal*, 22(June–July), 493–520.

Anderson, L. (2002). In search of the perfect web site. Smart Business, (March), 60–64.

Bakos, Y. (1997). Reducing buyer search costs: Implications for electronic marketplaces. Management Science, 43(12), 1676–1692.

Brynjolfsson, E., & Smith, M. D. (2000). Frictionless commerce? A comparison of internet and conventional retailers. Management Science, 46(4), 563–585.

Cameron, M. (1999). Content that works on the web. Target Marketing, 1(November), 22–58.

Chen, P.-Y. S., & Hitt, L. M. (2000). Switching cost and brand loyalty in electronic markets: Evidence from On-line retail brokers. In W. J. Orlikowski, S. Ang, P. Weill, H. C. Krcmar, & J. I. DeGross (Eds.), *Proceedings of the*

M. Del Giudice, M.R. Della Peruta, *The Satisfaction of Change*
DOI 10.1007/978-3-319-41884-1

Twenty-First International Conference on Information Systems (pp. 134–144). Brisbane, Australia, December 14–17.

Christopher, M., Payne, A., & Ballantyne, D. (1992). *Relationship marketing*. London: Heineman.

Cialdini, R. B. (1984). *Influence. How and why people agree to do things*. New York: W. Morrow.

Clemmer, C. E., & Schneider, B. (1996). Fair service. *Advances in Service Marketing and Management, 5*, 109–126.

Cronin Jr., J. J., & Taylor, S. A. (1992). Measuring service quality: A reexamination and extension. *Journal of Marketing, 56*(July), 55–68.

Crosby, L. A., & Taylor, J. R. (1983). Psychological commitment and its effects on post-decision evaluation and preference stability among voters. *Journal of Consumer Research, 9*(March), 413–431.

Cummings, L. L., & Bromiley, P. (1996). The Organizational Trust Inventory (OTI). Development and validation. In M. R. Kramer & T. R. Tyler (Eds.), *Trust in organizations* (pp. 302–330). Thousand Oaks, CA: Sage.

D'Aveni, R. (1994). *Hypercompetition*. New Yok: The Free Press.

Deighton, J. (1996). The future of interactive marketing. *Harvard Business Review, 74*(November–December), 151–162.

Del Giudice, M., & del Giudice, F. (2003). Locking-in the customer: How to manage switching costs to stimulate e-loyalty and reduce churn rate. In S. K. Sharma & J. Gupta (Ed.), *Managing e-business of the 21st century*. Heidelberg: Heidelberg Press.

Del Giudice, M., & Maggioni, V. (2014). Managerial practices and operative directions of knowledge management within inter-firm networks: A global view. *Journal of Knowledge Management, 18*(5), 841–846.

Del Giudice, M., & Polski, M. (2003). *Having to be loyal or wanting to be loyal: The role of the website on customer churn and retention*. New York: International Business Information Management Association.

Doney, P. M., & Cannon, J. P. (1997). An examination of the nature of trust in buyer-seller relationships. *Journal of Marketing, 61*(April), 35–51.

Ford, D. (Ed.) (1990). *Understanding business markets: Interaction, relationships and networks*. London: Academic Press.

Gambetta, D. (1988). *Trust. Making and breaking cooperative relations*. Oxford: Basil Blackwell.

Ghosh, S. (1998). Making business sense of the Internet. *Harvard Business Review, 76*(March–April), 127–135.

Grisaffe, D. B., & Kumar, A. (1998). Antecedents and consequences of customer value: Testing an expanded framework. *Working Paper 27* (pp. 98–107). Cambridge, MA: Marketing Science Institute.

Hagel III, J., & Singer, M. (1999). Unbundling the corporation. *Harvard Business Review, 77*(2), 133–141.

Hakansson, H., Johanson, J., & Wootz, B. (1976). Influence tactics in buyer-seller processes. *Industrial Marketing Management, 5*(6), 139–164.

Hakansson, H., & Osteberg, C. (1975). Industrial marketing: An organizational problem? *Industrial Marketing Management, 4*, 113–123.

Hart, S., Smith, A., Sparks, L., & Tzokas, N. (1999). Are loyalty schemes a manifestation of relationship marketing? *Journal of Marketing Management, 15*, 541–562.

Hartman, A., & Sifonis, J. G. (2000). *Net ready: Strategies for success in the e-conomy*. New York, NY: McGraw-Hill Publishing Company.

Hax, A. C., & Wilde II, D. L. (1999). The delta model: Adaptive management for a changing world. *Sloan Management Review, 40*(2), 11–28.

Hax, A. C., & Wilde II, D. L. (2001). *The delta*. New York, NY: Palgrave.

Hoffman, D., Novak, T., & Chatterjee, P. (1995). Commercial scenarios for the web: Opportunities and challenges. *Journal of Computer Mediated Communication, 1*(3), Special Issue on Electronic Commerce.

Hoffman, D. L., & Novak, T. P. (1996). Marketing in hypermedia computer-mediated environments: Conceptual foundations. *Journal of Marketing, 60*(July), 50–68.

Holbrook, M. B. (1999). *Consumer value*. London: Routledge.

Houston, F. (1986). The marketing concept: What it is and what it is not. *Journal of Marketing, 50*(April), 81–87.

Howard, J. (1977). *Consumer behavior: Application of theory*. Boston: McGraw Hill.

Jaworski, B., & Kohli, A. (1993). Market orientation: Antecedents and consequences. *Journal of Marketing, 57*(July), 53–70.

Johnson, M. P. (1982). Social and cognitive features of the dissolution of commitment to relationships. In S. Duck (Ed.), *Personal relationships: Dissolving personal relationships*. London: Academic Press.

Jones, M. A., Motherbaugh, D. L., & Beatty, S. (2000). Switching barriers and repurchase intentions in services. *Journal of Retailing, 76*(2), 259–274.

Jones, T. O., & Sasser, E. W. (1992). Why satisfied customer defect. *Harvard Business Review, 73*(November–December), 88–99.

Kalakota, R., & Whinston, A. (1997). *Electronic commerce. A manager's guide*. Reading, MA: Addison Wesley.

Kaplan, L. B., Szybillo, G. J., & Jacoby, J. (1974). Components of perceived risk in product purchase: A cross validation. *Journal of Applied Psychology*, (May), 16–28.

Katz, M. L., & Shapiro, C. (1985). Network externalities, competition, and compatibility. *American Economic Review, 75*, 424–440.

Keaveney, S. M. (1995). Customer switching behavior in service industries: An exploratory study. *Journal of Marketing, 59*(April), 71–82.

Kiani, G. (1998). Marketing opportunities in the digital world. *Internet Research: Electronic Networking Applications and Policy, 8*(2), 185–194.

Klemperer, P. (1995). Competition when consumers have switching costs: An overview with applications to industrial organization, macroeconomics, and international trade. *Review of Economic Studies, 62*, 515–539.

Kosiur, D. (1997). *Understanding electronic commerce*. Redmond, WA: Microsoft Press.

Novak, T. P., Hoffman, D., & Yung, Y. (2000). Measuring the customer experience in online environments: A structural modeling approach. *Marketing Science, 19*(1), 22–42.

Oliva, T. A., Oliver, R. L., & MacMillan, I. C. (1992). A catastrophe model for developing service satisfaction strategies. *Journal of Marketing, 56*(July), 83–95.

Palacios-Marqués, D., Merigó, J. M., & Soto-Acosta, P. (2015a). Online social networks as an enabler of innovation in organizations. *Management Decision, 53*(9), 1906–1920.

Palacios-Marqués, D., Soto-Acosta, P., & Merigó, J. M. (2015b). Analyzing the effects of technological, organizational and competition factors on web knowledge exchange in SMEs. *Telematics and Informatics, 32*(1), 23–32.

Soto-Acosta, P., Casado-Lumbreras, C., & Cabezas-Isla, F. (2010). Shaping human capital in software development teams: The case of mentoring enabled by semantics. *IET Software, 4*(6), 445–452.

Soto-Acosta, P., Popa, S., & Palacios-Marqués, D. (2015). E-business, organizational innovation and firm performance in manufacturing SMEs: An empirical study in Spain. *Technological and Economic Development of Economy*, 1–20. doi:10.3846/20294913.2015.1074126

Straub, D. W., Hoffman, D. L., Weber, B. W., & Steinfield, C. (2002a). Measuring e-commerce in net-enabled organizations: An introduction to the special issue. *Information Systems Research, 13*(2), 115–124.

Straub, D. W., Hoffman, D. L., Weber, B. W., & Steinfield, C. (2002b). Toward new metrics for net-enhanced organizations. *Information Systems Research, 13*(3), 227–238.

Zwass, V. (1998). Structure and macro-level impacts of electronic commerce: From technological infrastructure to electronic marketplaces. In K. Kendall (Ed.), *Emerging information technologies*. Thousand Oaks, CA: Sage Publications.

Index

Note: Page numbers with "n" denote notes.

M. Del Giudice, M.R. Della Peruta, *The Satisfaction of Change*,
DOI 10.1007/978-3-319-41884-1

The manufacturer's authorised representative in the EU is Springer Nature Customer Service Centre GmbH, Europaplatz 3, 69115 Heidelberg, Germany. If you have any concerns regarding our products, please contact ProductSafety@springernature.com

Printed and bound by CPI Group (UK) Ltd, Croydon, CR0 4YY

30/09/2026

02225609-0008